FLOODLAND AND FOREST

Memories of the Chilliwack Valley

Imbert Orchard

SOUND HERITAGE SERIES   Number 37

CHARLES LILLARD, Editor
DEREK REIMER, Head, Sound and Moving Image Division

Published by the SOUND AND MOVING IMAGE DIVISION

Province of British Columbia

Ministry of
Provincial Secretary and
Government Services
PROVINCIAL ARCHIVES

© 1983 Provincial Archives of British Columbia
Victoria, British Columbia

Cover: Looking north on Mill St. during the Chilliwack flood of 1894. B. S. Bradshaw is in the boat; Roy and Alex Chadsey are on the raft. Norm McGillvray is on the right next to the dog and Don McGillvray stands behind him (PABC 10337).
Inside front cover: The first detailed map of the area that later became the townsite of Chilliwack.
Inside back cover: Frederick Walter Lee, Lane, Shannon Mt. Road, Chilliwack, watercolour (PABC, pdp 4427).
Back cover: Dr. J. C. Henderson; the Vedder bridge is in the background (PABC 43235).

Canadian Cataloguing in Publication Data

Orchard, Imbert.

　　Floodland and forest

　　(Sound heritage series, ISSN 0228-7781 ; no. 37)

　　ISBN 0-7718-8343-9

　　1. Chilliwack region (B.C.) — History. 2. Chilliwack region (B.C.) — Biography. 3. Oral history. I. Provincial Archives of British Columbia. Sound and Moving Image Division.
II. Title. III. Series.

　　FC3845.C5072　　971.1'33　　C83-092042-0
　　F1089.C5072

CONTENTS

FROM THE MIDDEN OF HUMAN MEMORY	iv
MAN AND NATURE	1
THE NEWCOMERS	8
COMMUNITY	23
NEW OPPORTUNITIES	43
FLOODWATERS	55
TOWN AND COUNTRY	65
SOURCES	83

From the Midden of Human Memory

This work is based on 15 tape recorded interviews with people of the Chilliwack area. I recorded them almost 20 years ago in the course of collecting material for a radio series about early days in the Lower Fraser Valley. Recently, when I began to fill in the historical picture from other sources, these oral memories came into focus as containing valuable statements of fact, or telling of happenings not recorded elsewhere. Above all, I saw them as opening windows on the thoughts, feelings and attitudes of a pioneer society. Such insights, from the midden of human memory, can be every bit as pertinent to our understanding as facts of the usual kind.

At the time when I interviewed these people my scope was limited. I mainly wanted to hear about life before the First World War. With radio programs in mind, I selected these interviewees, not simply because they were available at the time of my visit, but because they had a reasonably good recall, as well as voices clear and pleasant enough for broadcasting.

Some were able to remember things that their parents had told them, but none of their firsthand memories went further back than the 1880s. To remedy this, I have made use of excerpts from written memoirs of the 1860s and 1870s, which often read as if they had been spoken. The most important of these were recorded by Horatio Webb, who came to the Chilliwack Valley in 1870, and was well acquainted with all the earliest settlers. (I was able to interview his sister, Kate, when she was 101.) Another useful account was written by Mary Kipp (Mrs. Isaac Kipp), who came from Upper Canada as a bride in 1865. In addition, it has been my good fortune to have been allowed access to the lively, conversational reminiscences of John Francis McCutcheon, who, like most of the other contributors, belongs to the second generation.

These memoirs, written or recorded, are supported by historical narrative or commentary; but it will be obvious that the work as a whole makes no pretence at being a comprehensive local history. Discussion is limited to the broad lines of development and to a mere handful of the more prominent people and their families. Of necessity, it touches but briefly, and only from a specific point of view, on the equally important life of the native peoples of the area.

Many thanks to Nora Layard, curator of the Chilliwack Museum and Historical Society, for her assistance, and also to D. R. Lind, Editor of the *Chilliwack Progress* for letting me see microfilm of the early editions, and for giving me permission to quote from various articles. My special thanks to the Chilliwack Museum and Historical Society for the use of their extensive and well-kept archives. I also acknowledge my debt to those cordial old-timers and others, who opened their doors to an inquisitive man from the CBC—and in particular to Oliver Wells for his friendly interest in what I was doing, and for contributing, before his untimely death, so much to our understanding of the history of the Chilliwack Valley and its native culture.

Imbert Orchard
Vancouver, December 1982

MAN AND NATURE

A sense of place

My discovery of the Chilliwack Valley began quite early one morning in 1942 when the train I was on ambled out of the Fraser Canyon on its way to the coast. The steep slopes fell away on either side and shortly after, for a space, I saw level farmland, ringed by mountains of many shapes and sizes. It was spring, and I remember that the cottonwood trees along the river were a delicate green. A month or so later I was living under canvas at a basic training camp in that same valley.

What comes to mind much more readily than the tribal rites of initiation into the Canadian Army, are some of the joys of the surrounding country during two months of glorious summer weather. We would be roused before the sun had appeared from behind the nearby hills; it would be shining, nevertheless, on the high fine-weather clouds that feathered the limpid blue of a Pacific sky. In spite of the ennui of army routine, it was a sight that never failed to raise one's spirits. The war seemed very far away. Weekdays would be spent marching up and down and learning the parts of the Bren gun, but the evenings and weekends were ours, and we were free to explore. Just up the road was the village of Sardis with its country store, its Indian hospital and surrounding hop fields. The latter reminded me of boyhood days in Kent, whereas the large barns and silos, and the ample farm houses, with their shade trees and verandahs, made me think of my native Ontario, although I didn't know then what the connection was.

Down the road from the camp was a wooden bridge crossing a fast flowing river, which no sooner emerged from the mountains than for some strange reason it changed its name. From there the road led up through a beautiful stand of fir and larch to Cultus Lake, of particularly happy memory. I had not yet been told that *cultus* means "bad" or "worthless" in the old Chinook jargon of the coast.

I remember my introduction to the rain forest, as I and others from the camp tried to climb to the top of Mount McGuire, struggling for hours through thick entanglements of bush and devil's club, over endless fallen tree trunks of enormous girth, and meeting up with

Frederick Walter Lee, *Fraser Valley*, watercolour (detail) (PABC, pdp 4420).

trails that had once been the roadbed of a logging railway. We came across a tiny prospector's cabin, and rumour had it the owner was a recluse, who worked his own little secret gold mine somewhere up Tamihi Creek.

To escape from it all, in those days we boarded one of the B. C. Electric's old trolley cars at Sardis and rattled down to Vancouver and the Carroll Street Station. And the journey back in the evening seemed an almost endless three hours, as we were rocked from side to side on seats too hard to sleep on, under lights too dim to read by, stopping almost everywhere.

And not till the very end of those months did it rain. By then there were forest fires on the slopes of the hills, glowing in the dark like the sabbath of a thousand witches. This, too, was part of the whole experience.

All this happened over 40 years ago, and I'm aware that these memories are overly romantic, even superficial. Twenty years later, when I returned and got to know some of the people who lived there, especially the old-timers, the picture acquired both depth and meaning. Yet, my initial affection for the place remained; and I renew it every time I drive up the freeway and, just past Abbotsford, find myself travelling along the edge of a plain that was once a large shallow lake. Then, as the road bends northward around Sumas Mountain, the full extent of the Chilliwack Valley comes into view, accented by clusters of buildings—mostly dairy farms—and a scattering of Lombardy poplars. It conveys to me a sense of place, something easily comprehended reaching south and east to the sudden slopes of the mountains, north to the Fraser River, its western edge defined by the ghostly shores of that same Sumas Lake. Small wonder even the earliest settlers were able to feel themselves pleasantly contained within those natural boundaries, when all beyond was a sea of unknown mountains.

A second Eden

In 1858-9 the International Boundary Commission was in the area laying out the boundary with the United States. The British party had a depot near the mouth of the Chilliwack River. Two of its members, seeing the valley in its primeval glory, went into raptures about it. "I think this is the most beautiful place I was ever in," wrote Lieutenant Charles Wilson in his diary [Wilson; 41]*. And John Keast Lord, the Commission's naturalist, had this to say: ". . . we pitched our tents on the edge of a lovely stream. Wildfowl were in abundance; the streams were alive with fish; the mules and horses revelling in grass knee-deep—we were in a second Eden! . . . The scenery is romantic and beautiful beyond description. Towering up into the very clouds, as a background, are the mighty hills of the Cascade range, their misty summits capped with perpetual snow—their craggy sides rent into chasms and ravines, whose depths and solitudes no man's foot has ever trodden. . . . The Chilukweyuk river . . . washes one side of the prairie. Silvery-green and ever-trembling cotton-wood trees, ruddy black-birch, and hawthorn, like a girdle, encircle the prairie, and form a border, of Nature's own weaving, to the brilliant carpet of emerald grass, patterned with wild flowers of every hue and tint—all shading pleasantly away, and losing their brilliancy in the dark green pine-trees" [Lord; 315, 341–42].

The picture is right out of J.M.W. Turner. And these were travelled men, familiar with many a beautiful landscape. The naturalist goes on to paint another scene, with the eye of a Paul Kane. "Before me, stretching away for about three miles, is an open grassy prairie, one side of which is bounded by the Chilukweyuk river, the other by the Fraser. At the junction of the two streams, at an angle of the prairie, stands an Indian village: the rude-plank sheds and rush-lodges; the white smoke, curling gracefully up through the still atmosphere from many lodge-fires; the dusky forms of the savages, as they loll or stroll in the fitful night, give life and character to a scene indescribably lovely" [Lord; 347].

---

* See Bibliography, p. 85: Charles Wilson, "Journal of Service," p. 41.

Oscar Humpheys and a friend atop Vedder Mountain;
below them are the Chilliwack floodlands (PABC 50445).

Charles Wilson recorded how he rode over to Sumas Lake with Lord ". . . to see if the water had fallen . . . it would have been a very pleasant ride, if we had not had pouring rain the whole day; our road lay through forest with occasional small prairies, on which the fern and grass grew to such a height as to hide both horse and rider. . . ." [Wilson; 51]. A few days later he wrote about ". . . a long ride on a very winding trail through forest and prairie. . . ." that took him up to Cultus Lake, only he called it "Schweltya," an approximation of its proper Indian name. The whole area was criss-crossed with Indian trails, and there were numerous serpentine waterways, some of which were navigable by dugout: the Luckakuck, for instance, and the Atchelitz, and the Sumas River on which one might travel into Sumas Lake and beyond.

In those days the big river, the Chilliwack, on escaping from its narrow mountain valley, swung to the north before it joined the Fraser. Yet, not many generations before, say the Indians, it was emptying itself due west into Sumas Lake. Indeed, at one time or another the river's delta system involved almost all the creeks and sloughs of this boggy plain. For when it's in flood, which can be either in the spring or the fall, it brings down sediment and all sorts of debris. In former times the sediment would settle and build itself up, and eventually acquire a covering of cedar trees. On the other hand, uprooted trees and shrubs could suddenly pile up at the head of one of the outlets, forcing the current to find another channel. So, according to Robert Joe, the Indians called the river Tswelmuh. "*Tswel* means 'go away,' " he said. "A river that changes its course." [RJ]*

Such was the unstable situation the European settlers had to contend with when they came to farm; but, of course, it had never bothered the native people very much, as they were considerably more mobile and adaptable. Moreover, they had very different notions about the ownership of land.

---

* See Interviews, p. 84: Robert Joe.

Cultural horizons

Archaeologists think it probable that there were people in the area 25,000 years ago, having come down from the north. If so, they would have been driven further south by the advance of the last of the great ice floes, which extended well down into what is now the State of Washington. By the time it had started to recede, probably some 14,000 years ago, all elevations below 5,000 feet in the area of the Chilliwack Valley had been worn to a roundness. About 11,000 years ago a relatively cold period returned, and the glaciers advanced again. But after another 500 years or so, when they had finally withdrawn, the whole floor of the valley, depressed by the great mass of the ice, had become a fiord of the sea, reaching from Bellingham Bay almost to the present town of Hope; and people had begun to move in again.

We know this because of archaeological discoveries of the early 1960s in the Fraser Canyon, just above Yale. The man in charge was the late Dr. Charles Borden, then Professor Emeritus of Archaeology at the University of British Columbia. He told me how they had been able "to develop a cultural sequence of seven phases and support it by radiocarbon dates, encompassing 9,000 years until the historic period—one of the longest sequences anywhere in the New World. "We had no idea," he said, "that occupation of this area extended back that far. And it has important implications, because the interior had not become ice free until just about the time when the earliest occupation occurred there; and this very strongly suggests that the people came from the south. They were descendants of people who had survived south of the ice front and were moving into British Columbia again."

The discovery of these middens has resulted in a new awareness of the evolution of cultures in this area, as well as of the great age of the human presence itself. Layer upon layer, phase upon phase of Stone Age knives, scrapers, choppers, projectile points and such, have told their story to the archaeologists. And all because of the salmon. Said Dr. Borden, "This particular locality is a very narrow stretch of river, where the salmon have great difficulty in making their way up; they have to utilize every eddy, you know, to rest up, and then make another short spurt up stream, and so forth. In some places I've stood in the water with fish all around my legs, and if I'd wanted to, all I had to do was scoop them out." The great annual migration reaches the vicinity of the canyon in the latter part of the summer, and by then their flesh is lean and in its prime. All the natives had to do was heave them on to the bank with spears or nets, slit them open and hang them up to cure in the canyon's steady wind. And so for countless centuries they gathered here from all around the Lower Fraser Valley, and even beyond. Today they call themselves the Stalo or River People, Stalo [*sta'lu*] being the Halkomelem word for a river.

In this vast and fishy cornucopia—the five miles of canyon that was Stalo territory—each tribe would have had their own hereditary fishing grounds; and there would have been guardian spirits to see to it that tribes like the Cowichan and the Musqueam, who in more recent times, we are told, could be rather warlike, refrained from molesting their more gentle neighbours of the Upper Stalo—at least for the duration.

Most of these same gentle people, when the fishing season was over, withdrew to their homes in the valley below, the Pilalt to the northeast corner of the Chilliwack plain, the Sumas to around Sumas Lake and the prairie to the west of it, while in between them were the Chilliwack, who claimed a large section of the plain all the way to the mouth of the Chilliwack River. They, nevertheless, built their villages along the upper valley, well within the mountains, fearing attacks from the coastal tribes or those at the head of Harrison Lake.

It is thought by some that the Chilliwack were not properly Stalo people at all, but came from over the mountains to the south; and their dialect was said to be related to those of their neighbours of the interior, the Skagit and the Nooksack. But no one today can speak it. No one even remembers it.

The Stalo now speak the Halkomelem language, which originated on Nicomen Island, just below Chilliwack; a soft sibilant language in keeping with their watery environment. As for the name "Chilliwack" or "Chilliwhack," it belongs to the old, forgotten language, and is one of the many native words that the white people have bent to their own stubborn tongues. The Fort Langley journals made mention of the "Chilcocooks" or the "Chiliqueyooks," meaning the tribe. Lieut. Wilson, coming a bit closer to the proper sound, spoke of the "Chilukweyuk stream."

According to Robert Joe it has two meanings, very common meanings, too. "You know, if there's a creek or a river, it goes just so far. That's *Tsil-khway-uk*, that's "as far as we go." "Or *Schil-khway-uk*," on the other hand, "is the head of a man or the head of a people."

It's alive

We have heard how one romantic Canadian and two romantic Englishmen reacted to the valley on first coming into it. What the native people felt, and perhaps still do, was quite another matter. It was part of the complex, vital, interplay between themselves and their surroundings.

> The white people stop to pray;
> we stop to respect—
> the same thing you know.
>
> We respect the woods,
> the living trees in the woods.
> We drink the water;
> it's alive.
> We breathe the air;
> it's alive too.
> Respect it!
>
> And it seems like everything you respect
> helps you along in life,
> what you're gonna try and accomplish, you see.
> That's the teaching of our old peoples there.   [JL]

What Joe Louie is saying to me is this: everything around you is alive. You are a partner in a world of give and take which demands mutual respect, mutual acceptance: between one human being and another, between humans and animals, humans and vegetable life, humans and the winds, the water, the sky and the earth itself. The Indian was on a person-to-person relationship with animals and other natural phenomena.

> I want to tell you about the cedar,
> the mother tree of the forest.
> You make your snowshoes out of its branches,
> you make your canoes, you make your baskets,
> make your housing out of the cedar,
> you can make your plates, the long plates
> that the Indians used long time.
> Everything was made from that mother tree.
>
> Whenever you're caught in a storm
> you get under a cedar tree.
> It's always dry underneath
> because the limbs is there.
> That's why the old people called it
> the mother tree of the forest.
> They respected that tree.   [JL]

Keeping watch over the Chilliwack Valley is the mother mountain—at least, that's the meaning of its Indian name: Theeth-uhl-kay. We call it Mount Cheam, perhaps because some early settler or Hudson's Bay man, pointed to it and asking what it was called, was given the name of the Pilalt village at its foot. Cheam [*ci'a.m*] means "wild strawberry place."

> That mountain was a person at one time, a woman. She had children. They are all sittin' behind her, and the youngest, a little girl, asked the mother, "I want to be in front of you so I can see people travelling on the river. "So she set the baby in front of her, you see. You can see it sticking out from the big mountain.   [DM]

For the Stalo, as for all the native peoples, the whole environment was speaking, as it were, with human tongues. Their story tellers led you into a land where trees and rocks and animals transformed themselves into people, and back again, until you couldn't be sure what's what. In like manner, the boundaries between the visible world and the invisible were equally uncertain. The latter revealed itself in visions, or to people with special powers. A certain body of water, a certain part of the woods, could be the habitat of strange unnatural creatures known as a Slalakums—possibly a giant snake, a two-headed monster, a cannibal woman, or that hairy giant we call a sasquatch. Cultus Lake was a *slalakum* place—a bad place. Anyone foolish enough to go swimming there could be eaten by the Bear-that-Lives-under-the-Water.

Among the more benign inhabitants of the Stalo's complex world were his guardian spirits, his *sulia,* usually associated with the vital force of some particular animal, and it was from these that he acquired many of his songs and dances, as well as the powers necessary for his role within the tribe. Such were of special concern to medicine men and hunters.

Indian salmon cache, possibly near Yale, B.C. (PABC 79711).

The deer sacrificed himself

Only today, now that our depredations are coming home to roost, can we begin to appreciate the Indian people's innate feeling for the balance of nature, and what they mean by "respect." Here, for instance, are two stories about hunters: one from the days of the early settlers, the other, although from quite recent times, takes us back into a very different world.

>Jack Wilson said one day he was riding along the old Yale Road past Bellrose, and he counted nine deer lying along the lakeshore in a distance of half a mile. You see, Bill Campbell and his friends were having a deer hunt that day. He had 30 hounds and he would turn them loose on the Vedder Mountain. The hounds would chase the deer, and the deer would hit for the lake, and the hunters would pick them off as they came down. No gamewardens in those days.   [JM]
>
>The old peoples respected this here life—like a deer or a bear, seems they're a livin' soul. They know that we're here and we have to help one another. Like me, I'm goin' out there to get some meat, deer meat there for my peoples. I get out there, and it seems like sometime it's really a good cause—if I'm gettin' it for a graveyard cleanin', you know, somethin' like that. And I get out there and it seems like they're waitin', and I respect it. The deer knows that he's going for a good cause, and he gives himself up—or a bear or anythin' like that. But say I take the meat that I had and just destroy it—that deer meat there, or that fish, or whatever it is. If I don't respect this here sacrifice or use that properly, it will be hard for me to get that again. I may be punished, maybe for a week, two weeks, something like that. So I have to respect. I have to teach my peoples, "This is part of the thing that keeps you alive. You have to respect it."
>
>It was just over a year ago, my boy that I raised here went up to the hills, and he says, "You know, I just got out of the car and walked up there, and there was a deer comin' right towards me," he said. "It looked like he was after me. So I shot him, and he dropped right there. So," he says, "I got it and put it on and took him home."
>
>I says, "What are you huntin' for? A funeral?"
>
>"Yes."
>
>"Well," I says, "the deer sacrificed himself."
>
>"I never thought of that," he says.
>
>I says, "Yeah. That's what we were taught. I thought I told you that before.
>
>"No," he says, "I guess, if you did, I forgot it."   [JL]

And so it fades—that age old wisdom—and with it the whole meaningful environment of legends and unseen forces, spells and visions, Slalakums, ghosts and guardian spirits. The valley itself, almost all of it now, is a white people's midden, where for over 120 years they've been shedding the artifacts of their own everyday life—their letters and diaries, official documents and newspapers, their drawings, photographs, tape recordings—year after year, layer upon layer. Such is the stuff of history, which only began in these parts, so we have decreed, when the first whiteman to appear on the scene took out his pencil and made an entry in his journal.

THE NEWCOMERS

Beaver country

The great river, the stalo, was the highway for salmon and men. It was the trade route when dried salmon and goats' wool blankets were bartered for wild potatoes and seal skins. It was the warpath of the Cowichan and their allies, coming to prey on the tribes of the upper stalo. And one day it brought down through the mountains members of a strange new tribe never encountered before, except by some of the coastal people.

Year by year the intruders had been making their way westward along the great rivers of the continent in canoes and bateaux, and up and down the coast in ships. When Alexander Mackenzie reached tidewater near Bella Coola the gap was closed, and it was only a matter of time—15 years to be precise—before another party found its way down the great river itself, surviving its fearful rapids and canyons, to the quieter waters of the lower valley. Then, because of the good graces of the Tait people, who lent them canoes, they were able to journey on to tidewater.

"Continued our course with a strong current. . . ." wrote Simon Fraser in his journal on 30th June, 1808. This was highwater time, and many of the islands and other floodlands would have been under water, so that somewhere near Agassiz he noted that ". . . the river expands into a lake. Here we saw seals, a large river coming in from the left," which can only have been the Chilliwack River itself, "and a round Mountain a head [sic], which the natives call *shemotch*" [Fraser; 102]. This mountain was probably the one we call Sumas. "After sunset we encamped upon the right side of the river. At this place the trees are remarkably large. . . . Musketoes are in clouds, & we had little or nothing to eat" [Ibid].

A few days later they were on their way back, and nothing of that nature disturbed the valley's equilibrium for another 16 years, when a party of Hudson's Bay people under Chief Trader McMillan came up from Fort Vancouver on the Columbia to confirm the whereabouts of this other large river. They worked their way up as far as Hatzic Lake, were most impressed with what they saw, and found the local people friendly. Three years later, McMillan returned with 23 men and built a depot on the south bank, which they named Fort Langley. They fortified it with the customary palisades, bastions and cannon, and from time to time sent out parties to explore the surrounding country. They were therefore the first whitemen to investigate the Chilliwack River complex and Sumas Lake.

As much of it was beaver country, they were eager for the natives to start trapping for them, but there was a problem. The marauding Cowichans and their like kept the local people in "Continual alarm" as the writer of Ft. Langley's journal of 19 March 1828 put it. "While the powerful tribes from Vancouvers Island harass them in this manner little hunts can be expected from them" [HBC; 63]. It was understood that the Company would have to support them against the "lawless Villains." Perhaps the new fort itself was a deterrent, because in 1831 there was a marked increase in the harvest of pelts. About that time, too, the Chilliwack people felt secure enough to set up villages closer to the Fraser.

It was the Company's policy to maintain, as far as possible, friendly and uncomplicated relations with the tribes on whom its wealth depended. They must not be disturbed in their native ways; and outsiders, be they independent traders or would-be settlers, were in general discouraged. Trading, itself, was nothing new to the Indians; but change of some sort was inevitable, if only because they had always been adaptable, within the limitations of their isolation, and had acquired a new currency. Their pelts now brought them guns, ammunition, woolen blankets and implements of iron. They no longer needed to manufacture tools and weapons out of their environment. For them the age of wood and stone was over.

On the one hand they were learning rapidly, on the other, bit by bit, they were coming to depend, not only on the whiteman's tools, but on the people who supplied them. For their part, the Hudson's Bay people were almost equally dependent on the natives, able to move among them peacefully only because of their friendship or tolerance. They learnt to accommodate themselves to local ways, and took native wives after the custom of the country. As a result, between 1827 and 1858, there was comparative stability in the Lower Fraser Valley, and a mutual give and take.

The Company established a farm on the flood meadows we now call Langley Prairie; and this would have introduced the Indians to the wonders of crops and cattle. They quickly learnt how to grow potatoes for themselves, finding them to be more prolific and nutritious than the wild roots they were accustomed to.

In 1839 the fort was rebuilt three miles up the river and close to the farm. Then, in 1846, when Britain surrendered her claims to all the mainland south of the 49th parallel, Fort Langley began to be seen as a depot for the fur brigades of the northern interior, provided a suitable trail could be developed through the rugged coastal mountains. By the end of 1849, when one had been finally constructed, the company established a post where it came down to the Fraser River. They named it Fort Hope, and from there every spring a procession of bateaux or canoes dropped swiftly down the river to Fort Langley, flags flying and laden with furs.

Those white people were starving

One wonders how long this quiet regime could have slumbered on in the valley, simply minding its own business, had it not quite suddenly been turned topsy-turvy by events beyond the control of either native or trader. This time the newcomers came in the thousands and found, practically underfoot, the currency for a new economic order. The California gold rush in 1849 had been followed a few years later by one in Australia, and now it was the Fraser River's turn. Small quantities of gold dust had already been collected in a variety of places on the mainland, particularly by the Indians. In 1857, when some prospectors, who had worked their way up the Okanagan Valley, came across rich deposits on the banks of the Thompson, the news quickly reached the ears of the Californians, and a new rush was on. In the spring of 1858, the Americans of Washington Territory were at war with the local Indians, so the majority of the miners had to come up the coast on crowded steamers, land in Victoria, and make their way across the Strait of Georgia in anything that would carry them; and, as we know, there was gold in the gravel bars all the way up the Fraser from the mouth of the Harrison River to the "Falls of the Fraser," as they called the canyon. But the important diggings began at Murderer's Bar, a few miles below Fort Hope, and Hill's Bar just below Fort Yale was the richest of all.

Every prospective miner was required to pay a license fee of 21 shillings a month, the equivalent of $5, and a gunboat was periodically stationed near the mouth of the Fraser to keep tab on all who entered. Those who considered this an unwarranted imposition landed at the little American settlement of Whatcom at Bellingham Bay, and backpacked up what was known as the Whatcom Trail. They would have crossed the border near the southwest corner of Sumas Lake, swung around to the east and arrived at the Fraser near the mouth of the Chilliwack River. There they would have come upon the winter trail the Hudson's Bay traders had cut out for themselves between Fort Langley and Fort Hope.

The Whatcom Trail, alone, would have taken the better part of a week to negotiate, as it was probably little more than an improved Indian trail. By the time the traveller arrived on the banks of the Fraser, worn out from his struggle with swamps, huge fallen trees and, in summer time, hordes of mosquitoes, his condition was often pitiful. The impression made on the Chilliwack Indians has lasted to this day.

> When I first hear them speaking about a white man, *Kwah-lee-tum,* that's what the Indians call the white man, because in them days those white people travelling on the way to the gold rush, they were starving. *Kwah-lee-tum,* that means "starving." Well, the Indians began to feed them, feed them till they get all right. They say the

Indians here in this valley, the Chilliwack Valley, are about the kindest Indians that's living—that's what the white people said.   [DM]

Danny Milo wasn't so complimentary about the Indians that lived further up the river.

They got way up the canyon. At that time there was no road at all, just little trails for the Indians to travel on. Well, those Indians got mean and they drowned a lot of them that was walking through that trail. My father used to tell me every once in a while he'd see a man drifting down the river with a pack.   [DM]

Danny Milo told me this in the spring of 1963, when he was said to be 99 years old, and since he was the youngest of 12 children it's entirely likely that his own father did witness the gold rush. But whatever else his father may have told him about battles with lawless Californians, he was too polite to say that many of them deserved what they got.

As the Chilliwack Valley with its open prairies was just down river from the gold bars of the Lower Fraser, many an erstwhile farmer must have wondered about its agricultural possibilities. However, the distinction of being the first to cultivate its soil goes to the natives. Lieut. Wilson of the British Boundary Survey party wrote of riding to Cultus Lake through thickly timbered land and passing "through magnificent Indian potato fields," which he regarded as evidence of the excellence of the soil. The first to bring livestock into the valley were undoubtedly those same survey people. They had moved in during the summer of 1858 with horses and Mexican mule trains, and also, it seems, with some beef cattle and a cow or two to provide milk. This means they would have put up fences; and we know that they built at least two corrals in which to winter their animals. They also must have cut and stored wild hay for winter feed. Miners coming up the Whatcom Trail in the summers of 1858 and 1859 and encountering one of the commission's camps, would have noticed how well their livestock were doing. Two of them, at least, that came that way—Volkert Vedder and Reuben Nowell—returned a few years later to take up land. But it's thought that the first man to obtain legal title to land in the Chilliwack Valley, was Jonathan Reece.

Fine pasture lands

Reece had been raised on a farm in Oxford County in what was then Upper Canada, and in his early twenties had come out to the gold fields of California. It is not reported how he made out, but four years later when he heard about the Thompson River strike, he took a ship to Victoria and landed there in April, 1858 to find thousands of other miners camped among the oak trees. He was able to buy a large Indian dugout for $200 in gold dust, quite a sum of money for those days. He loaded it with six tons of provisions and then, with the help of five other men, paddled it through the islands and across the strait to the mouth of the Fraser, where he met up with the gunboat and had to pay "the sum of FIVE DOLLARS in payment of one month's license in advance," so read the receipt given him by the collector. The ex-farmboy must have taken note of the rich water-meadows of the delta and the other patches of prairie that here and there interrupted the seemingly endless forest. Years later he remembered that no one had yet disturbed the cedar trees where New Westminster is today, whereas the banks at Fort Langley and Fort Hope were crowded with miners' tents. As his party continued their journey towards the canyon, and they picked up the bodies of no less than 17 whitemen, some with arrows sticking in them, some decapitated. Horatio Webb, a friend of Reece's, in later years, said, "he mined at Emory [Emory's] Bar that winter and spring with fair success."

Relatively few made their fortunes. The majority worked very hard in abominable conditions for very little, or nothing at all, hoping that tomorrow or next week or further up the river they would strike pay dirt.

In their wake came a throng of equally eager merchants, packers, liquor vendors, innkeepers and so on, seeking their fortunes in their own way; and some of the miners,

Volkert Vedder
(PABC 37369).

Jonathan Reece
(PABC 29381).

giving up hope, reverted to being axemen, blacksmiths, packers, harness-makers, butchers, bakers, gamblers and thieves—according to the need. Sometime during the summer of 1859 Jonathan Reece opened a butcher shop at Fort Hope in partnership with John Lawrence. No doubt, fresh beef, pork or mutton, when it was available at all, would have been brought in on the hoof on the deck of a steamboat, and the animals pastured or corralled on the Hope flats until they were slaughtered. The partners, however, had a better idea. Reece took the ship for Oregon and the Willamette Valley, where he bought 200 head of fat three- and four-year-old steers at approximately $20 a head. He drove them north to Seattle, where he put them on a steamer, and they were taken to Whatcom. As the village lacked a wharf, the cattle had to be put in a sling, one by one, hoisted over the side, and made to swim ashore. Then they were driven up the Whatcom Trail.

> Coming into the Chilliwack Valley with his cattle he was so taken up with its fine pasture lands that he decided to leave the greater part of them there, with a man by the name of Alex Ling in charge, who drove them to Fort Hope as they were needed. They had five dogs to assist them in driving the herd; two each side of the trail and an old bulldog on the trail. In case any of the cattle got troublesome and wanted to go back, two of the dogs would go at their heels and the old bulldog would grab them by the nose, often throwing them to the ground. They were generally well behaved after this treatment. Mr. Reece valued his dogs far more than any steer.   [HW-1]

This is how Jonathan Reece may have become the first person to take up land in the valley. For, according to Horatio Webb, who had come to the Valley in 1870 to work for Reece, and so knew him well:

> He was the first man to pre-empt land in the Colony of British Columbia, having taken up his land in 1859 and had to send to England for his deeds*.   [HW-2]

---
* This statement is doubtful; the land rights were controlled by the HBC, not the British government. The colony did not establish the *Pre-emption Act* until January 4, 1860.

But to begin with there was little, if any, cultivation. Reece was simply running his cattle on the open prairie, and others were doing much the same thing. Volkert Vedder, for instance, who is said to have come up the Whatcom Trail in 1856, went back to California and returned in 1862 with his sons, Adam and Albert. Apparently they brought in some cattle or oxen with them, because they camped for a while on Sumas Prairie before getting into the freight hauling business on the Cariboo Road. In the summer of 1861 Reece made another trip to Oregon; this time he came back with 300 head and left them for the time being with the Vedders.

> Mr. Reece paid dear for leaving his cattle on Sumass Prairie for in November 1861 from four to five feet of snow fell soon after a heavy crust formed making it almost impossible to move the cattle to Chilliwhack where he had some hay.
> He lost over two hundred head out of his herd that he brought from Oregon that summer dying along the trail from starvation he told me it was a hard sight to see these big steers lay down and die when so near to feed [Webb; 5–6].

Sometime in 1862 the partners moved their butcher shop to Yale, because newer, more powerful river steamers had made it the head of navigation. That fall two of Jonathan's cousins, Isaac and James Kipp, came down from the goldfields, their money gone, and looking for work. So they were sent down to the ranch to take care of the cattle.

> Coming down from Yale this trip the steamer went up the Chilliwack River to what was always known as the Mark's place. Mr. Kipp told me when the boat landed he found two men living there, Thomas Marks and Matthew Sweetman, both living in a tent on the banks of the Luckukuk. They went back down the river as far as Squihala leaving the boat and taking the Hudson Bay trail to the log cabin on the Reece place where they found Alex Ling in charge. He left in a day or two, and they never saw him again. . . . In driving the cattle to Yale they had an ox for a leader named Lamb. He was a wonderful ox. (Many a time I have ploughed with him.) He would take the lead and when they came to a stream of water was always ready to take the lead, even to the old Fraser. . . . From Yale they would start him back alone and he would swim the Fraser and other streams, getting home in two or three days. . . . Later on Lamb was killed by Mr. Reece on his farm, for beef. He was good and fat and I shall never forget how when the neighbours sent for a piece of beef Mr. Reece always doubled the weight ordered. He said it was a trick of the trade.   [HW-1]
> In 1864 a wagon road was built from Yale to Cariboo, a distance of 400 miles. The freight was carried by mule teams, ox teams and pack horses—four to six span of mules in a team, which were driven with a single jerk line, the oxen generally seven to eight yokes in a team. They only made one trip in a season, and would not leave Yale until about the middle of May and get back the latter part of October. When they came down in the fall, they were always very poor. They all wintered their oxen on islands in the Fraser River adjacent to [the] Chilliwack [Valley] on rushes which grew in abundance on these islands. There was two kinds: a fine rush grew eight to ten inches high and very thick on the ground; another variety grew four to five feet high and much coarser. These rushes were excellent fooding value. In the spring these poor old oxen would be good beef.
> The first few years we wintered all our cattle, young and old on these rushes and they always came out in first class shape. They would get in the woods under the big cedar for shelter. We always had a big time getting them out in the spring. We had to swim them across the Fraser, big droves of them. . . . Different farmers who owned the cattle would send a man each. Sometimes we would take our blankets along and some eats and camp for two or three days with a foot of snow on the ground, but we could always find a place to camp under some cedar tree. We always took salt for them. Some of the cattle were pretty wild but would always come for the salt. . . . We had an old ox that was a wonderful good leader. He would take the water like a

duck and the others would follow. Sometimes there would be over 100 head of all ages, always some calves, two or three months old, but they always made it. The Fraser River is swift and sometimes they would drift down nearly a quarter of a mile.   [HW-1]

Reece and Isaac Kipp were the first men to register cattle brands in British Columbia. At New Westminster on February 2, 1870, Reece and Kipp recorded their "JR" and "K" brands.

Wild horses couldn't hold him

Isaac and James Kipp—they were cousins, not brothers—decided to take up land for themselves, and so, together with Reece's partner, John Lawrence, they preempted lots immediately to the north of Jonathan Reece's place and proceeded to farm their land collectively. It was a choice location, easily accessible from the river and, being slightly raised above the surrounding land, not normally subject to the annual flooding. The eastern portions were timbered, with scrubby or open prairie to the west.

> Messrs. Kipp having been brought up as farmers, soon got to work ploughing the new land. The ground was very uneven and on most knolls was a clump of either nut hazel or birch. They often got their plow stuck fast in these roots and had to take off their lead team to pull the plow loose. They used a large plow with 24-inch share and seven yoke oxen. The first harrow they used was made with wooden teeth which had to be replaced a good many times, the teeth often breaking. Ploughing the ground so deep the first time, so as to get below the roots as much as possible, the first crop was not very good, but after cultivation it improved.   [HW-1]

Reece and his cousins, the Kipps, had been neighbours back in Upper Canada. The family farms were clustered near the border between Oxford and Brant Counties, not far from Woodstock, and the nearest settlement was a tiny place that in those days went by the name of Centreville. Their parents were all United Empire Loyalists. Reece's father was born in Germany, but his mother was a Kipp, and the Kipp ancestors were Dutch, who for more than 200 years had been moving westward. And now, Jonathan, Isaac and James,

Isaac Kipp (PABC 6163).

closely followed by Isaac's younger brother, Henry, had reached the continent's western limits. Jim Kipp, Henry's son, liked to tell it this way.

> They came from Holland first, and they landed at that Plymouth Rock, and then they went over into Flatbush District—I don't know how far they are apart—but, anyway they drifted from there into Pennsylvania. And they were coming west, even in those days. Well, in 1812, I think it was, the Americans picked a row with Canada, and these people wouldn't fight against the Canadians. So they says, "Out of here you go, then!" So they chased them out. And Pennsylvania is not very far from Ontario, you see; it borders on Lake Erie. So they went over to Canada, these Dutchmen that came from Holland. There was two brothers, Isaac and Benjamin. [JK]

The gist of Jim Kipp's story is doubtlessly correct, even if his sense of history is a bit fanciful. It is recorded that the first of the family's emigrants, Hendrik de Kype, landed in the new world in 1637, and Flatbush on Long Island was certainly a Dutch settlement. But in point of fact the brothers came to Canada somewhat earlier, as a consequence of the War of Independence. Two generations later, in December of 1858, Isaac Kipp, a lad of 19, and his cousin James, turned up in the gold fields of northern California. By then, Jonathan Reece was already on the banks of the Fraser. Isaac's younger brother, Henry, joined them the following year, enticed it would seem, by the colourful letters Isaac was writing home.

> He was just a youngster in his teens, 16 or so. He wouldn't stay there any longer, not in Ontario, than he could help. He had to work from morning to night, and he never got any pleasure to go anywhere at all. He told me that they had to have all the work done by the 24th May. There was generally a big circus came through the country at that time. It would land there in Woodstock, and they could go to the circus *if* the work was all done. But if the work wasn't done he stayed home. And they never had any money to spend, nothing at all—just work, work, work, like slaves. All the schooling he ever got was three years. He'd go in the fall when it would freeze up and they couldn't work outside anymore. Then as soon as it came time to make maple sugar, out he'd come and go into the sugar bush, and had to make the maple syrup and the sugar.
>
> Oh, yes! Wild horses couldn't hold him in there when he heard what a rosy thing it was out in the west. Because his two older brothers, Isaac Kipp and Hamilton, they were out there already making their fortunes and they sent him some money to make his getaway with*. He talked the neighbour boy into going along with him, and the two of them ran away and went to New York and down the Atlantic coast on a sailing vessel and docked at Panama. And, strange to say, there was a railway across that Panama in those days. Then they got on a steamer and came up to San Francisco; and I don't know how he got up to Marysville, but that's where the gold rush was on, and that's where they were headed for. [JK]

One account has it that he walked to Bakersfield, which is in quite the opposite direction from Marysville. At any rate, he joined his brother Isaac. But when Isaac and James moved on to British Columbia, Henry stayed behind and, whatever he was doing, managed to hang in there till 1864. Jim Kipp's story about Henry's leaving is true to form.

> The American army—I suppose they'd be the Northerners—they gave orders that they were getting the worst of it in the Civil War, and they said, "You join up and help us fight, or get out again." So he thought he was a Canadian, he wasn't an American, he'd go back to where he came from on the Canadian side. He got to Victoria, and then he came across to New Westminster. Then he got on the steamer and came up to Yale. It was the head of navigation; they couldn't get any further, and they can't yet. [JK]

---

* Hamilton Kipp was Isaac's older brother, but it was his cousin, James, who went to California with him.

By then the Cariboo Road had been completed, and stage coaches were running. But when he heard that the passengers had to walk up every hill, he thought he might just as easily walk down the hills as well. So he went on foot all the way from Yale to Barkerville carrying his pack and his violin.

> He learnt to play the violin when he was a youngster, and he brought that with him from his home. And he used to play it in the dance halls up there, and he'd get $25 a night. And then he'd hunt gold in the daytime, and he was making a fortune fast. [JK]

But not from mining. However, as one report puts it, "he did have experiences," and for two years played his fiddle in 'Professor' Carpenter's orchestra for $25 a night.

The cattle were just rolling fat

By this time there were others beginning to settle in the valley wherever good land was sufficiently accessible; that's to say, if it was near a trail or one or other of the little rivers or sloughs. We get some idea of these beginnings from an article in The *British Columbian* of September 19th, 1866. They sent somebody to look at what the newspaper called "The Agricultural Interests of the Lower Fraser," and he found that in the Chilliwack Valley ". . . a good deal had already been accomplished." 4,860 acres of land had been taken up, of which 653 acres were under cultivation; that season 818 tons of hay and 12,770 bushels of grain had been cut, and 5,200 bushels of potatoes and 2,800 bushels of turnips had been grown. There were 744 head of cattle in the valley, as well as 425 hogs and 1,207 poultry.

Only two of the farms were noted as being in their fourth year of operation. One was the Marks and Barber farm, just south of the Chilliwack River; the other belonged to Volkert Vedder, who had located on the Whatcom Trail close to what came to be called Vedder Mountain. But neither were among the more advanced producers. Adam and Albert Vedder had gone into the freighting business on the newly completed Cariboo Road. In fact, it was Adam Vedder who drove the first ox team through to the Cariboo in 1865. When the Cariboo excitement faded the sons had returned to the valley and taken out preemptions adjoining their father's, and the whole was operated as one large farm. Adam Vedder was remembered by the old-timers as the one "who really stayed here and became quite an outstanding citizen, after whom the Vedder River, Vedder Mountain and all that was named*." [NP]

The most advanced farm, according to the 1866 article, was the 800 acres of the Kipp and Reece partnership. By that time, Isaac and Henry Kipp, the farmers, and Jonathan Reece, the butcher, had bought out the other partners. James Kipp had gone home. "He got too much high water and mosquitoes," said Jim Kipp, "and he went back to 'God's Country', as he called it—back to Ontario. He'd had enough of this western atmosphere." The newspaper stated that 350 of their 800 acres were now under cultivation, fenced with 40,000 rails. There were large sheds and barns. They had 340 head of cattle and 20 horses, and had cut 165 tons of hay. They were raising hogs and poultry, growing quantities of potatoes and turnips, as well as the usual garden vegetables, and had 20 acres of corn. Besides selling a lot of butter and eggs, they had manufactured 1,500 pounds of cheese ". . . of a quality superior to the best brands being brought in from the States."

This is an impressive beginning for a farm only in its third year of cultivation. It would seem that, prior to the arrival of Isaac and James in 1862, very little had been done with the land, except as a place to run beef cattle. It also indicates that the butchery business was profitable enough to pay for all the hired help they would have needed.

Adjoining them on the east was the farm of Reuben Nowell who had once been a professional gambler. He was one of the Americans who had come in via Whatcom to avoid

---

* According to the *Biographical Dictionary of Well-known British Columbians (1890)*, Adam Vedder arrived in B.C. in 1860, via Panama, and "built the first house ever erected . . . and occupied the first pre-emption recorded, in either Sumas or Chilliwhack." There is an unsubstantiated story that it was Adam, not Volkert Vedder, who first came to the valley.

being taxed. He had followed the trail all the way to ". . . the forks of the Thompson River . . . [and] was all through the Cariboo gold excitement in '62" [*Chilliwack Progress*; 14 May 1891]. On the far side of him was James Bertrand, another American. He'd been working on the boundary survey, and Volkert Vedder had spent the night with him the first time he came through the valley. All of these homesteads were north of the Chilliwack River, between there and the Fraser, straddling the Whatcom Trail and the old HBC trail to Hope; and all would, one day, be swallowed up by the city of Chilliwack. West of them was Indian territory and the Landing where the steamboats came to pick up produce.

When Henry Kipp decided to give up his musical career in Barkerville and join his relatives, he divided his time between the butcher shop and the farm.

> He used to look after the cattle. He said that the rushes, great tall green rushes, would grow and be green all winter long, along the edges of these streams that were running around in this low boggy place, and that the cattle were just rolling fat there. They'd eat these things when there was snow on the ground. And then he would drive the cattle up to this Jonathan Reece and help kill them, I suppose, till they were used up. And then he would come back and get another lot.   [JK]

After a while Henry Kipp started looking for land for himself. By this time all the suitable Chilliwack prairie had been taken up, so he had to choose between a preemption in the often swampy cedar forest, or one on the prairie at the far end of Sumas Lake. He chose the latter, but "the mosquitoes and the high water got so thick down there that he quit." [JK]

The farm he eventually acquired came to him under rather unusual circumstances. According to his son:

> A farmer was going down to the boat to get his groceries and mail and stuff. And he got into an argument with a stranger who happened to be there buying something, too. He got into such a heated argument that the stranger called him, "a damned whitewashed Yankee." That made him so mad he pulled out his six-shooter and shot the stranger—killed him right there on the spot. And then, when he realized—when he'd cooled off a little—what he'd done, he got right straight up and went down to my uncle's and sold his place to him for $500, and went home and got a rifle and some supplies, and lit out through the swamps at Sardis and got across the Vedder and went out to Cultus Lake and down into the States. And they never did catch him. Then they transferred my father from his share of this large farm and put him over on this 500 acre homestead that they bought; and that was our home then.   [JK]

> In 1869 Mr. Reece decided to give up the butchering business in Yale and move down on the farm, so they [the Kipps and Reeces] made a division of the stock and the land, Mr. Reece getting 210 acres on the west side which was mostly cultivated, some prairie but no timber, so he took 80 acres of timber on the east side. The Kipp brothers kept the center and the buildings. Mr. Reece's was the best land.   [HW-2]

Reece went down to New Westminster for the winter, and it was there that he ran into the young Horatio Webb. Raish, as everyone called him, was probably still in this teens when he left his native Bedfordshire for New York state. He seems to have had some idea about looking for gold in British Columbia, so he didn't stay there long—just long enough to fall in love with the daughter of the farmer he was working for. Since that was the year that the Central Pacific linked up with the Southern Pacific, and the first transcontinental railroad went into operation, he made his journey westward by train, and then by boat to New Westminster, where his sister, Sarah Ashwell, and her husband, George, were living. This was in the fall of 1869, and by then "the gold excitement was over and times were very quiet. Most of the miners having left the country."   [HW-2]

Sumas Lake; looking east to Vedder Crossing area (PABC 50451).

Ashwell was making and selling furniture, so Webb spent the winter helping out in the store. When spring came along, this eager, good-natured farmboy must have been quite ready to jump on a steamer and travel up to the Chilliwack Valley to work for Reece.

> The first work I did was to help dig a well. Mr. Reece had to build new buildings and we lived with the Kipps for some time until we could get a house built. Mr. Reece was a good carpenter and engaged another carpenter, and they soon got enough of the house finished so we could move into it: a kitchen, dining room and two bedrooms downstairs. The upper part was finished later. [HW-2]

The Lower Sumas settlement

At the same time as this little group of settlers around the mouth of the Chilliwack River was bringing their land into production, the large Chadsey family was putting down its roots on the more or less open prairie north and east of Sumas Lake. First to come were the brothers, Chester and James, together with their sister and her husband, David W. Miller—all from the shores of Lake Ontario. As that was in 1862, the Cariboo excitement was at its peak, so thither went the Chadsey brothers; but as Miller's wife was expecting, he settled her in Victoria before he too went looking for gold. After little more than a month, the brothers called it quits, hiked the 400 miles down to Yale and took the steamer to New Westminster. There they ran into a man who was looking for help in harvesting the wild hay on Sumas Prairie, and engaged to work for him. And while they were doing that, they fell so much in love with the place they decided to settle; so they built themselves a little cabin. David Miller, having returned equally penniless to Victoria, was persuaded to join them, and they all took up land and formed a partnership. Four years later two more Chadsey brothers arrived in the valley, bringing their parents with them. And so it came about that a large and happy family became the nucleus of the lower Sumas settlement. By 1866 they had managed to clear 80 of their 650 acres. That year they produced no small quantity of grain, hay, potatoes and turnips and put down 1,700 tobacco plants. They were annually making over 2,000 pounds of butter, which was sealed in tins and freighted into the interior by ox-team. It sold in the mining camps for $1 a pound.

Their brother-in-law, David Miller, seems to have had an eye for business. The report of 1866 notes ". . . he has sold his interest to the Chadseys and is about to remove to his own property, a beautiful place at the steamboat landing, where buildings and other improvements are now in progress." That same year, still dreaming of making a quick fortune, he took himself off to the Big Bend of the Columbia River where a minor gold rush was under way—again to no avail, as far as he was concerned, except as another adventure, another yarn. But the store he opened at Miller's Landing, the first store in the Chilliwack area, appears to have been a success; and every year he sold quantities of hay from his land.

A tree was just a tree

It is obvious that the mere act of looking for gold contributed little to the growth of the colony. While gold itself was a factor once it got into circulation, any real progress, as we understand it, was due to those who gave up as miners and settled in to practice some trade or talent they had acquired elsewhere. The drive and initiative that had led these ex-farmboys, and others like them, to exchange a comfortable family home for the raw wilderness of California or British Columbia, now led them to look for pay dirt of another kind and then make it work for them.

For them, it was a country without legend or tradition. They had left their ghosts behind them. A lake, however beautiful, was just a lake, a mountain a mountain, waiting for some surveyor to give it a name and measurement. A tree was just a tree—and probably in the way. As for animal life, they brought much of it with them, seeing it largely as a soulless commodity to be bred and slaughtered for profit. And whereas the aborigines filled their homeland with a throng of meaningful presences, white people, finding it was used only for hunting, fishing and gathering, simply saw an empty wilderness, awaiting the day when such as they would make it over—as a matter of right—in their own image.

This image as we know, originated in the eastern colonies and states. Only a small minority in the Chilliwack Valley had come from the older countries. The majority had grown up on the homesteads their own fathers and grandfathers had hewn out of the forest. So they knew very well the kind of social and physical environment they wanted to recreate, and what it would demand of them. They had acquired their know-how with their mother's milk, which is why they got so quickly on their feet; this, and having a gold rush almost at their back door. And this is why so few of them gave up in the early years of settlement.

For the Chilliwack Valley was lucky in its pioneers. They brought with them, not only their sturdy self-reliance, but the moral, economic and political leadership that would contribute to a stable community. One thinks particularly of men like A.C. Wells, who was described by his grandson, Oliver, as ". . . one of these strong characters, brought up under Methodism to believe what was right was right, and what was wrong was wrong—no in between." Besides being an ardent Methodist and one of the district's first JPs, he was a leading dairyman. Innovative, versatile, patriarchal—something of a local squire—yet Wells also went out of his way to be a firm friend and counsellor to the Indians. Allen Casey Wells, known to all the sundry as A.C., could trace his descent from New England colonists. An ancestor, Thomas Welles, and his son, John, emigrated from Somerset in 1636 to one of the colonial settlements that later became part of Connecticut. When John's great-great-grandson came to Upper Canada as a United Empire Loyalist, he took up land near Napanee and dropped the final "e" of his surname. A.C. was this man's grandson, and he and his brother were harness-makers at Newbergh. When he decided to try his luck in the Cariboo mines, he was 25 and already three years married. His grandson, Oliver, picks up the story:

> He came west at the time of the goldrush in 1862. He was going up the Fraser by Indian canoe, and according to some records he stopped and camped at the end of the Chilliwack River. But he went on up to the goldfields. He established one or two claims, one of which turned out quite well after he'd sold it; but he came out of the

goldfields broke, and came down to Yale. And at Yale he took up his trade. At that time the Barnard Express Company was operating out of Yale, and he made the harness for the first six-horse team that took a stage over the Cariboo Road. [OW]

In 1864 he was well enough established to send for his wife, and with her came his sister, Jane, and three other women. Jane married Charles Evans, the bookkeeper and dispatcher for the Barnard Express. Evans took up a large block of land bordering Atchelitz Creek, and arranged for his brother-in-law to start a farm there and look after it for him. That was how, in 1865, A.C. and his family—he now had a daughter—came to live in the valley. By the following year he had managed to put 55 acres under cultivation, and this had produced 2,000 bushels of grain and hundreds of bushels of potatoes and carrots. That fall he brought 50 cows up from Oregon to start a dairy herd, presumably.

Living in the valley, Wells was able to scout around for himself, and eventually, like some of the others, he acquired several lots.

> He bought the first property in the fall of 1866 from the wife of Sergeant McColl, who was one of the Royal Engineers. McColl had built himself a small frame house on it, and he died or was killed.
> When he first came in to locate the land he got an Indian to bring him up a stream that was known as the Kaytse-slyee, which has all been covered in since. And my grandfather came into an area which was not only kind of boggy, but it was a timbered area. Those already established thought he was foolish to go so far from the river, their only means of transportation, and also have to clear land, because the land which was adjacent to the river and flooded in highwaters was grassland. [OW]

> The land was wet, but Mr. Wells saw it could be drained. The streams had lots of fall, but they were stopped up with beaver dams. He got the Indians to trap the beaver, after which he cut out the dams and the channel soon deepened and he was soon able to clear and cultivate his land. . . ." [HW-1]
> Your cleared land, you'd try and save that for hay. And as you were clearing land you'd seed down your oats. And I remember quite well the cradle for cutting the oats. [CB]

> I well remember the first time I saw a grain cradle used. It was by Mr. Reece. He was an expert cradler. He had a field of three acres of oats and barley, a fairly light crop. He had a new cradle called a turkey wing. He took a good share of the forenoon to grind the scythe and fix the fingers to suit him. We had dinner that day at half past eleven. At the dinner table he made a bargain with me that he would cut the field of grain that day, if I would milk the cows, some fifteen or sixteen. I took him up quickly, and sure enough before dark it was all well cut, and I had the cows milked. It was a great treat to me to see how straight and even he laid his swath . . . our grain we would leave in the swatch to dry before binding it and then haul it into the barn without stooking it. Up to 1871 the grain was threshed mostly with horses trampling it out. [HW-1]
> I have seen threshing done by the flail—lots of it done by the flail here. In the winter time in the old barn they'd clean a space and thrash the grain.
> Everybody grew enough for themselves; there was no particular sale. It was mostly barter. As far as we were concerned—and I think we were about the same as the others—we would grow a little bit of wheat every year, enough to make our bread. It was all whole wheat flour. And there wasn't any difficulty in getting good things to eat; you had your garden, you had your fruit. It took only a few years before there was fruit; and there was a lot of natural fruit here, too, in the way of berries, besides game—any amount of game: grouse and ducks were in here by the million. And usually every year there was a pork barrel, or two pork barrels, put down. [CB]

Grandmother used to make candles, and her butter and soap. And we always had a great big barrel of corned beef, and a great big barrel of sauerkraut, and everything like that for the winter. [NM]

I know that we could grow carrots and spuds then—really exhibition stuff—without any trouble at all. They'd be beautiful big carrots and all clean. Today you've got worms in them, and spuds have got the blight, and everything you plant has got something in it. [JF]

In general, the virgin soil was rich and productive wherever they were, whether they had to hew and burn each field, acre by acre out of the cedar forest—five acres a year were considered average—or could put the plough without more ado to the grassland or scrub. The newspaper article of September 1866, finds the prairie specially attractive, ". . . and of a better quality and more extensive than we had supposed. The soil is rich clay loam, slightly undulating in many places and easily cultivated." The report goes on to state there are ". . . still many thousands of acres of this land inviting the settler."

As for the settlers who were already there, ". . . all of them," remarks the report, "have had to struggle against numerous obstacles, both natural and legislative." It calls for "a liberal and enlightened policy" in regard to the "adaptation of the bottom prairie land for supplying a large rural population," with an end to having "the millions now sent out of the country to buy foreign produce, retained in it and spent amongst us."

However, the following January—they'd had a mild winter, for a change—the newspaper was able to report ". . . numerous flourishing farms on the Sumas and Chilliwack, in the Langley district, as well as in the immediate vicinity of this city," and that the markets were plentifully supplied with "beef, mutton, pork, eggs, butter, vegetables and orchard products. . . . Now our farmers can, and do, supply our wants" [*Columbian*; 9 Jan. 1867].

The cattle raising, which had given the valley farmers their start, by the mid 1860s had to meet the challenge of the big ranches of the interior, but there was always a good market for hay and oats, which were particularly suited to the valley's climate. Hay, wild or cultivated, could be said to be the fuel of the horse-and-buggy age, and we learn from one article of ". . . the immense profit there was in this trade. The Sumas prairie was and had been for centuries untouched. Blue-joint grass grew so rank that five tons to the acre was often cut, and this has been sold at times, landed at the Sumas boat landing about half a mile distant, for $20 a ton, and oat hay for $50 . . . so that an idea can be had as to the price of fodder and produce when it arrived at its destination, toted overland three or four hundred miles by ox-team or pack-train. It must have compared quite favorably, pound for pound, with the gold dust of the Cariboo" [*Progress*; 25 June 1958].

Abe Willis farm, 1895 (PABC 60634).

Wild roses used to bloom at the top of the water

Much of this wild hay came from what was known as marginal land, the flood meadows at either end of Sumas Lake. This large, shallow body of water stretched all the way between Sumas and Vedder mountains and, until it was drained in the early 1920s, formed the western boundary of the Chilliwack plain.

There was between ten and twelve thousand acres of lake, and there was no depth to it. When it wasn't in freshet I don't think there would be an average depth of three feet, hardly—maybe four. There was always fish in it. There was some quite large sturgeon taken out of Sumas Lake when they drained it. In the fall it was a sanctuary for ducks; there'd be duck on there by the million, and they would come in to feed in the marshes around the edge of the lake at night; and for an hour at dusk, why, a good shot would get anywhere from 20 to 40 ducks in an evening, just shooting them in flight. That has all been more or less forgotten about. Since the lake was drained the ducks don't come this way any more, and it was quite a hunter's paradise in those days. The Indians used to paddle their canoes across it, but I only know of one pleasure boat, and that was an old sailboat the Bowmans had, and they used to go on picnics with it now and again.   [WF]

I would say there was five or six thousand acres that was marginal land that didn't belong to anybody. It was still government land; and that was still an attraction when we moved here. We used the marginal lands of the lake to cut hay or run a bunch of young cattle for pasturing. They had a kind of gentleman's agreement. If a man went out and cut a swatch around a certain tract of land, why, that was his hay. And nobody would infringe on his rights to that hay. Of course, it wasn't only the people that lived right close to the lake bed that used the marginal land, especially for pasture. There were people even as far away as the other side of Chilliwack that used to drive cattle down in the early spring and pasture them there. The water, as it came up, drove the cattle back, and they would take them home when they got up close to the farms. When the water went down, they would bring them back down again to pasture until their feeding time in the winter. So that benefited a lot of people.

Some of that land was privately owned, but to put a fence in you had to drive the posts with a pile driver, or the first water that came, the posts all floated out of the ground, and your fence was flat. But if you drove them with a pile driver they would stay. The next problem was that the driftwood that would be washed in with the water would break the wires. So these people that owned some of that marginal land didn't fence it, because they felt that they just couldn't keep up with the repair bill.   [FZ]

I suppose the most exciting thing we had was our annual high water. Some years we managed to weather the storm and not move off. We generally figured about once in five years we would have to move off.   [FZ]

It wouldn't inundate all of the prairie. It would be just the low places in it; and then there'd be the ridges all along where there was trees and that, and where many of these farmers had their farms.   [JF]

The lake would flood from here into Whatcom County and out to the sea through Whatcom.   [WF]

I've seen water three feet deep in a shoemaker's store in Sumas, Washington. And they had a boat to come up into the store.   [JF]

The high water was very pleasant to play around in and swim in, and it was a beautiful sight. Wild roses used to bloom just at the top of the water. And there was the very lovely perfume that came from them as the water came up to them—a sight that was pretty, even though it was disastrous. We made many rafts in those days, as well as using the wooden tubs to sail in. Children had a good time playing in the high water—till the mosquitoes came; then you didn't play very much.   [S]

Frederick Walter Lee, *The Vedder, Chilliwack,* watercolour (PABC, pdp 3783).

The stock got used to the flood, and would even go to the hills when the water was up; and then, as soon as the water receded they would take back to the flat again.   [WF]

Usually it went quite quickly—it didn't stay around too long. As soon as the water was gone, the grass started right in; and they would pasture their cattle and make hay on it again in very little time.   [RS]

When the water would recede then the mosquitoes were here in hordes and hordes. That area out there was the breeding ground for them. Oh boy, they were vicious! You'd actually breathe them; they were in clouds. Anybody that lived here at that time can bear me out on that. There was one year—I just forget the year—when all the women and children had to go to Vancouver or the coast; they couldn't stand it. They killed a baby out here on Sumas Prairie. The child had kicked the netting off the crib, and the mosquitoes got at him and killed him. And calves—many calves were killed by the mosquitoes; they were just smothered—you know, calves that were just born. You couldn't sit down and milk a cow, because they'd eat you alive, and the cow couldn't stand it. We had to give up milking—that's a fact!   [JF]

There was no screen doors in those days. You could get the cloth mosquito netting for the windows, but nothing for the doors. We lived with a smudge pot. If you sat by the door step to peel potatoes, or went out to the garden to gather your produce, you took your smudge pot with you. You know what a smudge pot is. You make a little fire in a big bucket, and then put clay over, or something, just so that it would smoke. I often wonder what any stranger coming there thought of us, because we must have smelt of smoke because we just lived in it.   [WR]

If you didn't wear shoes they chewed your feet off. The girls used to put papers in their stockings to keep their legs from being bitten, and we were all set to wear a veil and gloves in mosquito time. I can remember trying to weed mangels and you had to get so many clothes on you just about suffocated. So for about a month in the summer after high water it was pretty disagreeable. If you didn't get high water, you didn't get mosquitoes. But you generally got high enough water, even in ordinary times, until they dyked the lake out. We haven't been bothered with them since.   [WF]

COMMUNITY

Snake fences everywhere

As one would expect, the Lower Fraser Valley of those early years had its share of forest fires, and the settlers had almost no means of dealing with them. There was a particularly big one during the summer of 1868, which started in Oregon and went all the way up to the coast of Alaska*.

> From April to November that year no rain fell and for two months all travel was stopped on account of the dense smoke. I have heard the settlers say that for two months they did not see the sun, having to use artificial light during the day. The river steamers had to tie up for quite a while.   [HW-1]

In the fall of 1878 there was another outbreak of forest fires, but according to a newspaper report they seemed to be doing more damage to fences than to anything else. And when they were over, it was thought that ". . . the service they have rendered in clearing the land will far exceed the damage."

Inevitably, this "second Eden" Wilson and Lord were so enthusiastic about was, year by year, surrendering its primeval glory either to the axe or fire. It was now becoming a world of rutted trails, wandering from clearing to clearing; of houses and barns, all made of logs and shakes; of shapeless, untidy fields, some still covered with stumps, surrounded by forest or a scraggy row of trees; along the edge a scattering of roots and stones, and snake fences everywhere, made of split cedar about four inches square and twelve feet long.

> One of the first jobs I had was to haul rails out of the woods 3,000 of them. Mr. Reece had got the Indians to make them at $15.00 a 1,000. He told them he did not care how big they were so sure some of them were all I could about put on the wagon. He told me afterwards why he told the Indians that. He often made two out of one and sometimes three. We selected the smallest rails for the first three so as to make it pig tight. Our pigs [were] often running at large. If we were building a permanent fence we would put two stakes about three inches square at each corner and wired the top. I saw one of our neighbours build a half a mile a day. It was a long day; he went out about five o'clock and did not get through until after seven. I laughed when he told me he was going to build that fence in a day.   [HW-2]

During the 1860s and 1870s land was being taken up mainly along the creeks and trails. One group of settlers was clustered around the lower end of the Chilliwack River (Reece, the Kipps, Nowell, Marks, etc.), another on the prairie north and east of Sumas Lake (the Chadseys, Miller, McGillivray, etc.), and yet another along the Atchelitz and the Luckakuck (Evans, William Hall, Wells, Sicker, etc.). But the settlement was gradual; following the decline of the gold fields, a period of recession had set in. It was this that, in 1866, forced the two rival colonies to pool their impoverishment.

To begin with there were only two trails of consequence: the original Whatcom Trail and the old Hudson's Bay trail, which Isaac Kipp and others had widened for their cattle drives to Hope. There were narrow Indian trails, of course, some of them, like the one to Cultus Lake, even suitable for horseback riding. Then in 1865 a new trail was cut through the whole length of the Lower Fraser Valley by the Collins Overland Telegraph Company, which was setting out to link America and Europe via Bering Strait and Siberia. However, by the time it reached the Kispiox Valley, another company had succeeded in laying a cable

---

* However unlikely this may seem, it is based on a comment by Horatio Webb, and is supported by a newspaper account. Elsewhere there is no record of such a fire; probably a series of fires burning along the coast gave rise to this story.

across the Atlantic, and the Collins' line was abandoned, with the exception of the section between New Westminster and Quesnel. An Irishman, by the name of John McCutcheon, who had been working on it all the way, returned to the valley in 1869 to become the local telegraph operator and linesman. His son, Jack, tells us:

> He set up his instruments first in the house of Isaac Kipp. Later he bought out a homestead from a settler by the name of John Hardison, and married Caroline Morey, daughter of Sergeant Morey of the Royal Engineers. When I was a youngster the telegraph instruments used to be set up in our big kitchen, and the instruments would be ticking away while we were at our meals. And sometimes my dad would say, "Whist!" and we would listen, with the result that we became telegraphers, some more proficient than others. [JM]

It was unusual, to say the least, for a backwoods community of those days to be able to communicate with the outside world by telegraph. At the same time, it gave the settlers another trail, this one started across the river from New Westminster, and came all the way through the thick woods to Matsqui prairie. From there it went over into Upper Sumas, followed the Whatcom Trail around the foot of Vedder Mountain, then swung somewhat further to the east, crossing the Chilliwack River at the Squiala reserve. But there were no bridges, so travellers had to swim their horses across the rivers.

Trails such as these would have to be improved considerably before the settlers could put their wagons on them. According to the Methodist missionary, Thomas Crosby, the first real road in the area was made so the settlers could come together to hear him preach. "Early the following week a 'bee' was called to make a road, with pole bridges over the sloughs, between Sumas and Chilliwack. . . ." [Crosby; 179]. A few years later, however, the new provincial government started to build a through highway from New Westminster to Yale, which is known today as the Old Yale Road wherever it has survived. When it came down out of the woods into Upper Sumas, it followed the Telegraph Trail until it approached the Chilliwack River. Then it swung to the right through John McCutcheon's farm and crossed the river by a bridge, precisely where the main road into Chilliwack crosses today. It met the Telegraph Trail again at what later became the Five Corners at the heart of the present city of Chilliwack and followed the trail eastward.

This road, including the bridges, was completed in 1875—after a fashion. On July 31st of that year the *Mainland Guardian* commented, ". . . in spring and the late autumn a stray horseman may pick his way over it. . . ." but ". . . at the present time the portions not covered by water are being traversed by fire." It was at its best as a winter road, when the mud would be frozen and the snow deep enough to fill the potholes. Settlers could then bring out their sleighs, and make music with the sleighbells, pretending perhaps, for an hour or so they were back home in Ontario. Some winters the frozen Fraser itself became a highway.

> One time my father was called down to New Westminster on business. It was in the wintertime, and there was no wagon road and no nothing to get out. The river was froze over and the steamers couldn't run. So he had to use skates. They made their skates in those days out of an old file or rasp or anything. They would take that sharp end and bend it up, like in the front, so you wouldn't stub your toe. Then they'd sharpen those files up—put them on a grindstone and grind them till they got sharp; and they'd make good skates They'd last a long while.

> And he got on these skates. He must have started real early, but he made it down there by around dinner time. On the road down there he found a deer, a great big one, and it had tried to get across on this ice, and it had slipped and straddled itself out. Actually it couldn't get up nor anything at all. So he cut its throat. The first Indian ranch he came to he told them about it, and they went back and got it for food. He went on down to New Westminster on skates. In one day he made that trip down there. [JK]

Presents for the bride

One would give a good deal to be able to read the letters sent home from the lonely cabins, written laboriously by candlelight after a long day's work. Did they tell about floods, mosquitoes, forest fires and rain? Did they speak about the beauties of nature, and how fertile land could be acquired for little more than the sweat of one's brow? Did they mention a longing for family and friends? Whatever was said, they managed to persuade the more venturesome of brothers, sisters and cousins, old friends and neighbours—and sweethearts, too—to come out to start a new life in this mountain valley.

In those days many a lad set out for the West with a girl in his heart, and very few of the young bachelors of the Chilliwack Valley married native girls. For the most part, they went back east to marry, or arranged somehow for their girls to join them. But in at least one recorded instance there was already a half-native family in the background, and the future bride, to her everlasting credit, refused to marry her man unless he promised to provide for them.

The first white woman in the area was David Miller's wife, who came in 1863; but Isaac Kipp's wife was the first to settle in Chilliwack. He and Mary Ann Nelmes had been sweethearts since their school days, and for seven years he kept in touch with her. When in 1865 she finally undertook the long journey, Isaac met her at New Westminster, and they were married. And Mary Kipp turned out to be everything that a pioneer woman should be. Before leaving home she had acquired some knowledge of medicine, and for 14 years was the only "doctor" in the locality. She was often called upon as midwife, and was universally respected and loved as friend, counsellor and foster mother to lonely young bachelors. When young Horatio Webb started to work for Jonathan Reece, helping him build his house, they all stayed at Isaac Kipp's.

> The first night I was put with an old Irishman to sleep. We slept in red blankets and I felt pretty homesick as it was my first experience sleeping in blankets. In the morning after milking I went to the house for breakfast which Mrs. Kipp was preparing for us. When I got there Mrs. Kipp's baby was crying. I took it up and played with it and it got quiet. That night I did not sleep with the Irishman. I had a bed to myself with nice sheets. Since that time I looked upon Mrs. I. Kipp like a mother. Her kindnesses to me in all these years I shall never forget. Many a lonely person of early days can tell of the many acts of kindness of Mrs. Kipp. Mr. Charles Evans in his book of poetry on Chilliwhack pioneer ladies calls her the Valley Queen and it has never been disputed [Webb; 9–10].

It required a lot of gumption in those days for a young girl like Mary Nelmes to come out on her own. The American Civil War was barely over and any sea voyage was hazardous, not to mention crossing the Isthmus of Panama. Chester Chadsey, the following year, picked up a bad case of yellow fever there on his way to find a wife. But by the time Horatio Webb was ready to marry the farmer's daughter in New York state, he could cross the continent by train all the way to San Francisco. Even then he didn't think he could ask her to travel alone.

> A visitor from Eastern Canada was staying at Mr. Kipp's and was watching us work . . . he asked Mr. Kipp why he didn't take a trip home to the East and see his folks. He had been away a good many years. Mr. Kipp replied he could not leave the farm. . . . "Get Webb to run it." So he asked me if I would. I told him if he would bring back my girl from New York State for me, never dreaming for a moment anything would come out of it. I went home with Mr. Kipp for dinner and this visitor brought up the same question at the dinner table, so Mr. Kipp said to his wife: "Well, Mary, could you and Raish run the ranch if I take a trip home." She said, "Sure we could manage it." As far as that goes she was quite capable to manage it herself. . . .

"Indian church and people at Methodist Church, 1890, Sardis." (PABC 39066).

> I got on fine. Got the hay and grain all harvested in good shape. I wrote to the girl and also her father and they both consented and Mr. Kipp went down to Norwich, New York State and took her up to his old home and the party started back. . . . I think Mr. Kipp must have told father Hopkins a pretty good story to get his consent to let her go as she was an only girl. [HW-2]

Also in that party were Isaac's brother, Alfred, with his wife and two children, a bride for his brother-in-law, David Nelmes, and two others. So a double wedding was held at the Kipps'.

Here is one more bride story. This one shows what could happen when she arrived.

> When he got a home to bring my mother to, my father [Henry Kipp] went east; and they married and came out together on the first transcontinental railway and landed in San Francisco. They came up to Victoria and up the river to Chilliwack. Well, the house wasn't quite finished when they got here, so she stayed with my aunt over here, Mrs. Isaac Kipp. And they were sitting one afternoon in the front room—I suppose they'd call it a parlor in those days—and all at once it got awfully dark. It was a nice bright day, too, and nice weather. And she looked around to see what was making it get dark and here the windows were all just filled with Indians looking at her. They knew him, he could speak their language, and they wanted to see what his squaw looked like. My mother was terrified. She thought she was going to get killed, that they were right after her. In the east they believed—they still believe—the Indians will scalp you out here, and you've got no chance for your life at all, unless you're careful. (Well, all the while I lived in the east they were talking that way. They thought this was a wild west show out here—they still think it is.)
>
> So my aunt says, "No." She says, "I understand a little of their language. I'll go out and tell them who you are."
>
> And so she did; and my mother went behind her, like she wouldn't dare go out there first. And here they'd come and brought a whole lot of presents for the bride, the new bride. She said there must have been two or three wheelbarrows full of their baskets and all this here ware that they made. Their things were piled up on this verandah out there for her to have. And my mother shook hands with them; that's about all she could do. She couldn't understand their language; she learned it afterwards. She could speak Chinook quite a bit, but she didn't know anything then. All she could think of was getting back in that house again and getting out of there. [JK]

This says a great deal about the relationship between the Indians and their new neighbours during the 1870s. By that time the Chilliwack people were all living in the lower part of the valley and sharing it with the much smaller band of Pilalt, who were scattered along the south bank of the Fraser. Eventually they were absorbed into the larger Chilliwack tribe. In all, there would have been little more than 300 Indians on the plain. They had always been friendly people; farmers like A.C. Wells employed quite a number during the haying and harvesting seasons.

The naturally good relationship had been aided by Governor Douglas' liberal policy of the 1860s in respect to reserves. He had instructed his surveyor to mark off reserves, not only around their villages, but wherever they had cleared and cultivated land, or had special ancestral claims. No reserve was to be less than 10 acres for every grown man, or less than 100 acres in all. And by the 1880s all the reserves in the valley had been officially surveyed.

As almost all this land was fertile, they could rent it out to the settlers or cultivate it themselves. Indeed having been cast out of their Eden, spiritually and psychologically, they had come to know good land from bad—even as the white man. They were even learning to assume his unoriginal sins. A letter from a Chilliwack Valley correspondent, writing for the *Mainland Guardian,* July 20, 1872, comments on the great change that had come over the Indians in the last ten years. They are now saving money, buying and raising stock, and cultivating gardens. It speaks of them ". . . serving to ape the whiteman in everything. . . ." They go to church, say grace at meals, pray night and morning; and all this is due to ". . . the energy and good advice of the Wesleyan methodists and the Jesuits [Oblates]. . . ."

Tablecloths were spread on the grass

It's not difficult to imagine what the arrival of the wives did for the quality of life. Where women and children were concerned, the small and unadorned bachelor's cabin was no longer adequate. It would have to be transformed in some way or allowed to become a shed or a pigsty, while something a bit grander was built.

>In the real early days when a settler wanted to build a log building, he would get all his material together there, and get it all cut and ready to put together. Then he'd invite all the neighbours; and everybody in the valley pretty well would come. And they'd bring along their wives with them, and something to eat. Then the women would stay inside and have a quilting bee, and have a regular visit; and the men would put the logs together and build this building. In the evening they would have a dance—these old time dances. They had all sorts of fancy dances in those days— square dances and everything you could think of, lots of dances we never hear tell of now.
>
>Then sometimes they would have a paring bee. They dried a lot of fruit in those days to carry them through the winter and cut down on their overhead. They would get some string, cheap cotton string, and they would make bit long strings of this fruit and hang it up over the stove to dry. Of course, the flies, they'd park there on top of this stuff, and I don't know whether they did any damage or not. Apples and pears they would do that way; cherries and plums they didn't bother with.
>
>And they would have a spelling match. They would get the smartest one that understood a dictionary to give out the words, and he would stand at the head of the room. Then they would choose captains for each side, and they would select people till they got enough to fill in, everybody in the room pretty well that wanted to take part in it. First one side then the other, they were given this word to spell. And if you couldn't spell it, you had to take your seat, and the first one that went down got a booby prize, some silly little thing that would make you sick to look at it. The last one got some nice book or clothing, or something that was really worthwhile. [JK]

The twenty-fourth of May was also a great day for all getting together; everybody went and took his basket. Tablecloths were spread on the grass, the food placed on them, and we took our places anywhere, as there were no reserved seats. We would have canoe racing, foot racing, and one year we all joined in a ring and played the old-fashioned drop-handkerchiefs or kiss-in-the-ring.   [HW-1]

But when summer came you didn't picnic too much. As Jim Kipp put it, "The mosquitoes were too thick. You couldn't sit still." Of course, there was a lot of getting together at Christmas and the New Year, with big community dinners. The Sumas people seem to have been the principal organizers in the earlier days. And there's a good story told about how, after ten years of these communal feasts, the wives had had enough, and decreed that henceforth every family should hold its own Christmas dinner. Whether this was considered to be rather more "high tone" has not been recorded, but the idea was so contrary to tradition that William Chadsey took it upon himself to be responsible for the dinner. So on Christmas Eve after working at his flour mill, he went in his sleigh from house to house—mainly those of his own relatives—purloining pies, puddings, geese, ducks and turkeys, and a huge Christmas cake that had been hidden in a piano. With the aid of the minister's wife, who worked all night, plucking and stuffing and roasting, everything was ready in time—not only the goodies, but tables and benches, all set up in the school house. Then, men on horseback rode hither and thither in the snow, summoning everyone to the valley's biggest Christmas dinner yet.

A lot of this hallelujah!

They built a church. The majority were Methodists, and the Methodist Church has a long tradition of itinerant preachers, able to endure the hardships of the trail and minister to isolated believers to a degree possibly equalled only by the Oblate priests. In such circumstances a church of any denomination was the centre of social, as well as religious, life and a cherished link with the civilized values of the outside world.

The first itinerant Methodist minister came into the area in the spring of 1865. He was Ebenezer Robson, a Canadian; from his diary and that of his successor's, Edward White, we learn that they preached at the homes of David Miller, Isaac Kipp and A. C. Wells. The latter was

> one of the strongest leaders of church and development in the valley, regardess of whether it was the Methodist Church. He even helped the Anglican Church get established. He was a strong contender for a great many things, which were for the

The Rev. Thomas Crosby
(PABC 5351).

benefit of the community. As a matter of fact, we found an old letter in the attic of his house. It wasn't signed, but it was a letter, which he'd made a copy from, requesting missionaries to be sent out by the Wesleyan Church in the old country.   [OW]

For two years the valley people were ministered to by Thomas Crosby, one of the outstanding early missionaries on the coast. His particular concern was the native people, and he spoke Halkomelem. The first time he came to the valley he paddled his own canoe all the way from Nanaimo, visited all eight of the native villages, and preached on Sunday at both Sumas and Chilliwack, presumably at Miller's and Kipp's. He is described as a big man with long arms, a heavy beard and a commanding voice.

> I think he was a very kind-hearted man, and to his friends and people who knew him he was very popular. But a casual stranger might get the wrong impression of him at a first meeting. He was inclined to be stern and abrupt, and whatever he said, he said it pretty strong; all of which were good qualities, I think, in those days. He was what you'd call a hell-fire preacher, and a lot of this hallelujah!—a lot of that.   [RW]
>
> The first church in the valley was a very small one on the banks of the Atcheliz Creek built in 1869. The first donation made towards that church was by an Indian chief; Atchlalah was his name. He gave Reverend Crosby a dollar and a half and he said, "That should start a drive to build a church for to worship in."   [JK]

In the spring of 1868 Crosby had conducted a camp meeting on the banks of this same creek, roughly half way between the Sumas and Chilliwack settlements. The place was described by the New Westminster paper as ". . . a pretty grove on the farm of Messrs. Evans and Wells." During the two days of the gathering a church board was set up: it decided the best place to build the church the Indian chief had asked for was right where they were. Although Charles Evans, the land owner, was not a devotee of emotional religion, like his brother-in-law, A. C. Wells, he gave them two acres. The little Atchelitz church was built that summer to serve protestants of several denominations.

Going to church could be a full day's occupation

> Most of the people attended church, some under great difficulties. Some went with oxen and wagons, some with horses and wagons, and some in canoes. . . . Those living to the east of the Chilliwack River would swim their horse across the river at Squihala.
>
> They would unsaddle at the water's edge, putting their saddle in the canoe and the Indians would paddle us across, guiding the horse by the side of the canoe. When Mr. and Mrs. Wells had two streams to cross, Mr. Wells would paddle the canoe and Mrs. Wells lead the horse, then they would haul the canoe, a very small one, across the land from one stream to the other with the horse, the rope hitched to the horn of the saddle.   [HW-1]
>
> I wasn't there, but they were telling me about it. They'd start early in the morning. My mother would always pack a great big milk can full of food, sandwiches and everything for to eat, and pie and cake. This man Ashwell—he was our next door neighbour—he would come and pick my mother and father up. And they'd get in the wagon, and the ladies would sit on chairs at the back, and the men would sit on an old sheepskin in the front of the wagon. It was the softest seat they could find; they didn't have any springs in the wagons in those days; and the roads were just like driving over a mountain, or next thing to it, awful rough, and mud holes in them. They'd go down here to my uncle's and tie the horses up, and feed them. Then they'd get into a canoe and go up this stream until they got to this little church where it crosses the highway there. Then they'd have a service in the morning and Sunday school in the afternoon. They'd take along eats, and have their dinner and maybe a little lunch after the Sunday school was over with. Then they'd get in this wagon and go home again.

One day they were getting into this wagon, and Ashwell, he had a young colt and an old horse—an old mare—hitched to the wagon. This colt was a nervous, jerky thing. And Mrs. Ashwell got up to fix something under her chair. She had her youngest child in her arms, and this young horse gave a jump, and away he went. She went over backwards, her and baby and all, into this mud puddle behind, and they landed right on their heads. My mother was setting down, so she didn't happen to go. [JK]

Thirty or forty years later several other centres would have their own little Methodist church: Sumas, Sardis, East Chilliwack and Chilliwack and there would be decent roads and bridges to get there on. Although by then the pioneer earnestness might have abated a trifle, in other respects the picture would be much the same.

Speaking of my own locality, Sardis, one of the big attractions was going to church. Everybody went to church. Today anybody that goes to church, they're regarded as a person that's a little bit more or less religious. But 40 or 50 years ago everybody went to church and nobody was considered too religious. Going to church was one way of meeting people you never saw any other time; and you'd get the news from the surrounding districts, what was going on. There was always considerable visiting, you know, before and after church. Everybody used to drive or ride saddle horse, and there might be a horse or two traded. Sometimes there was a little bit of fun after church watching some of the riders get on their horses and leave. There was generally a pretty good bucking horse or two there. Generally it was more of a social centre than it was a religious gathering. That's one reason why the churches were so well patronised in those days. [RW]

In 1873 the first Episcopal church was built in the valley. This church was first built at Fort Douglas by the sappers and miners. The lumber was whipsawed and hand-dressed. At a meeting held at the house of Mr. McCutcheon, in 1873, presided over by Bishop Hills of Victoria, whose diocese took in all British Columbia, an offer was made to us of this church with all its belongings. We accepted the offer and took steps to get it taken down and removed to Chilliwack. [HW-1]

People sometimes wonder why St. Thomas Anglican Church was brought all the way down from Fort Douglas. It was because Fort Douglas was being disbanded as a shorter route up into the Cariboo. The people here in Chilliwack had heard about this lovely church, which had been donated by Lady Angela Burdett-Coutts in England, and much of the material in that church had been sent out from England—beautiful oak and fixtures, and that kind of thing. When the bishop met with a few Anglicans here in Chilliwack, he told them if they felt there were enough Anglicans to warrant one, they could have this church provided they would bring it down. So they hired these Indians up at the Queen Charlotte Islands, the Haida tribe, and they made the finest canoes of all the coastal Indian tribes. And this church was taken apart and laced to six Haida canoes and brought down Harrison Lake, Harrison River and across the Fraser to Chilliwack, and was reassembled on a triangular piece of ground, donated by Isaac Kipp. Once they got it reassembled and the different furnishings all in place, they felt they had a very wonderful church. Back of the church it was all hazel and willow and alder, a few big trees and considerable brush, so it was in a very rough setting at first. [NP]

My father, he was raised in the Methodist church back there in Ontario. When they got out here—all that bunch from back there in Ontario, the Methodists—you couldn't say your head was your own. You had to get their idea of what you should do before you could do anything. And this got his back up. They built a church where the Christian Science is now, and they built another one at Sumas. It's still down there. Then the Presbyterians, the Scotsmen, got busy then, and they built the Presbyterian, because "We're not going to be dictated to, what we'll eat and what we'll do. We'll run our own show." So my father pulled out of this Methodist and went to the Presbyterians. [JK]

She would hear this weird crying

As the roads and trails became more passable, and as the clearings continued to expand, reducing the twilight zone that separated them, there was a growing sense of community. This was given impetus, of course, by the coming of the brides and wives, and the subsequent arrival of children. Churches and schools were built, and several stores were opened. At the same time people were beginning to look beyond the mountains. When Upper Canada, where most of them had been born, became Ontario and part of the new dominion, the valley stood strongly for confederation and in 1868 David W. Miller, representing the New Westminster district, was sent as a delegate to the Yale Convention, which had been summoned to challenge a balky Legislative Council. So there can be no doubt that when, on July 20th, 1871, confederation finally happened, there was much rejoicing.

The progressive people of Sumas were the first in the area to receive help from the new provincial government in building their school, but the Chilliwack people were not far behind. Mrs. Isaac Kipp recalled they were required to have no less than 13 children, but the official register for the first year shows there were only seven. "They went and got two or three Indian children—borrowed them," said Jim Kipp.

This school was not far from the Landing—"west of the old race track on the old Kipp Road," wrote Mrs. Kipp. "A teacher was engaged, and all went well for a few weeks, until one morning the children gathered, but no teacher came. He had heard the steamer whistle, caught it and was seen no more." "The mosquitoes were too much for him!" said Jim Kipp.

The next teacher, Alexander Peers, was a local farmer and brother-in-law of A. C. Wells. And it seems that as long as there was no bridge across the Chilliwack River, part of his class found it too difficult to get to school; so he taught the Chilliwack children in the morning, then swam his horse across the river and taught the Atchelitz children in the afternoon. The bridge on the new Yale Road must have been built by the following year, because attendance jumped to 24.

Another result of confederation was that, in 1873, the people of Sumas, Atchelitz and Chilliwack were able to form themselves into a municipality. At a meeting in the Sumas school house, John McCutcheon, the telegraph operator, was made reeve, the enterprising Jonathan Reece was made treasurer, and the clerk was Samuel Shannon. Among the councillors were David Miller and Henry Kipp. Understandably, their first concerns were with roads and bridges, to make it easier for people to get together. For instance, they felt a need "to construct the most necessary portion of the Yale-New Westminster road which runs through the municipality"—in other words, to turn it into a decent, ordinary wagon road, and one that could serve the new homesteads that were opening up in the heavily timbered area to the east.

Here were to be found several of those extended families, so typical of the valley—like the Gillanders, the Hendersons and the Ryders. John and Cory Ryder were from Upper Canada and had been freighting for the Hudson's Bay Company on the Cariboo Road, before deciding to take up land just east of Little Mountain in what was known as the Cheam district.

> My father, Cory Spencer Ryder, settled in the Cheam district in 1873 and took up 160 acres of land. We lived in a little log cabin right among the trees, heavy cedar and fir and hemlock and birch, and all that kind of thing, right up close, right around the windows. My mother asked my father why the windows were so small, and he said, "Well, if the cougars come sometime when I'm away they wouldn't be so apt to try to get in—or the bears—as they would if the windows were larger. So they were small windows up rather high. And when we were little children, and my father went to New Westminster—there was one day going down on the boat, and one coming back the next day—my mother would be alone there in the woods with her little people. (There were six of us born in the cabin without a doctor, and there were four born later on in the big frame house with Dr. Henderson, our pioneer doctor, in charge.) Mother said

Although used as a root house for many years, this cabin may be the oldest house in the Chilliwhack Municipality. It was built before 1865. Later it belonged to Charles Evans, then A. C. Wells lived in it while he was managing the Evans property (PABC 90818).

there were nights when my father was away when she would hear this weird crying out—like a baby crying, almost, and 'twas a cougar, just not very far back in the woods from the cabin. Then across Hope Slough, which was in front of our house, where the forest was about as dense, I think, as any part of the valley, another cougar would answer, and this weird wailing cry would come out. The one at the back of our place would cry out again. And she who had been born in England, and didn't even know there were such things as live cougars, said that cry was the most terrifying thing. She knew in a way that she was safe, but the tiniest little rustle of leaves outside, or anything like that, would just send her blood curdling, because she was afraid of these cougars trying to get into the house, because they would be very hungry.   [NP]

By 1874 the Cheam district had acquired a school and 17 pupils. A bit further to the east were the Hendersons, a large and somewhat confusing family, because they had several Johns, Arthurs and Isaacs. A. C. Henderson and his brother, Samuel, were originally from the north of Ireland, but had been living in Kansas. They came to the valley in 1875 for reasons of health and liked it so much that they brought in nearly all the rest of the family two years later. One exception was young John Cotter Henderson, Samuel's son, who was studying in the old country. He finished by attending medical school in Glasgow, and became the valley's pioneer doctor. The Hendersons called their place Rosedale.

Further east still, between the foot of Mt. Cheam and the Fraser River, was Popkum [originally Popcum], which took its name from a nearby Indian village. It sprang up in the mid-1870s, growing around the valley's first lumber mill, and soon became a thriving community. The mill was started by a man named David Airth; later it was taken over by the Knight brothers, William and Ebenezer. The area was thick with virgin timber, and the huge logs were extracted by teams of oxen. Water power came from Popkum Creek, but it's said that steam was used as well, for they produced not only lumber, but shingles and excelsior. The latter was used for packing china and glass, and for mattresses.

The whole operation was wonderfully self-contained. They had their own store, butcher shop, and, briefly, a post office. There was a blacksmith shop where they shod their oxen and repaired machinery, a tannery where they made their own belts and harness. Popkum even had a jail. They also had their own river-boat, "*The Lady Popcum,*" for taking their produce to market and bringing in supplies. The skipper and engineer was Bill Knight himself. On one occasion he took a boatload of ice down to New Westminster; ice that had been cut out of a slough in winter and stored in sawdust. Knight married Jennie Kipp, the 16-year-old daughter of Isaac and Mary, and the first white child born in the valley. Like her mother, she would take care of people and help them out with their problems, and was much beloved in her community.

One of the daughters of this William Knight told me in later years that one of the greatest events of the week at Popkum was when the boat landed and whistled. There would then be dead silence. Everybody listened as the sound of the whistle reverberated from Mt. Cheam and Mt. Lady Peak, and all down the Cheam range you'd hear this sound going, until it subsided.

Another thing she said was that the Indians—there was Long Louie and a gang of them—would bring the logs up over a skid road from out of the forest to the mill, and they would be dumped into the mill pond. And as the oxen would get opposite the kitchen window, Mrs. Knight would look out to see them coming. Long Louie had a vaulting pole. He would use it, I guess, with the oxen, guiding them or punishing them. As he got opposite the window he would let out this whoop and vault over the head yoke of oxen and land on the other side.   [NP]

They came because they were neighbours

With a sawmill in the valley it became possible to build something a bit better than a log cabin. But unless one could afford otherwise, it would still have to be simple, rectangular, reasonably functional, with a door in the middle and a window on either side. But above the door there could be a central gable, enclosing an upstairs window, as in eastern Canada. When the owner got more money, he might build a verandah on one or two sides, and a kitchen extension with outhouses, or add a little elegance with some fretwork ornament. All he required was a good carpenter, and a bricklayer for the chimney, and both were to be found in the neighbourhood.

So instead of those rough-hewn little log buildings, weathered and uneven, but quite at ease with the surroundings from which they were fashioned, the landscape came to be dotted with trim, white boxes, and equally trim looking sheds and barns with walls of vertical boarding. "We have emerged!" they seemed to say. Indeed, the whole pattern of roads and fences, gardens and furrowed fields, together with the new buildings, proclaimed that a sense of order had now been imposed on an unruly wilderness. Behind it all was the *Pre-emption Amendment Act* of 1861, which decreed: "Lands purchased as well as lands pre-empted shall be of rectangular shape, the shortest side being two thirds the length of the longest side. The boundaries shall as nearly as may according to the cardinal points of the compass."

Between 1868 and 1872 there was a sudden surge towards mechanisation. It started with the Chadsey brothers bringing in a reaping machine.

> A man rode on the seat at the back of the cutting bar and pulled the bundles off with a rake, the sheaves being tied by hand . . . the grain was threshed mostly with horses tramping it out. Mr. Reece had a home-made threshing machine that threshed out the grain but did not clean it. In 1871 the Kipp brothers with R[euben] Nowell and John Blanchard bought a Pitts threshing machine, ten-horsepower, which cleaned the grain ready for market. This was a great boon to us and encouraged the growing of more grain. For some years this machine did the threshing of the whole valley. [HW-l]

Shortly after came the first mower and cream separator, the latter brought in by A. C. Wells. In 1872 two of the Chadseys started a flour mill at Miller's Landing. "It was an old fashioned one," said Mary Kipp, "grinding with stones, one set above the other, but alas, our wheat was too damp and soft to make good flour . . . Mr. James Trethewey moved from Mission Creek to Elk Creek and built another mill, run by water power, and although he was a good English miller, the results were the same. So we continued to purchase our flour from Oregon" [*Progress*; 25 June 1958].

When I was a youngster we had nothing but whole wheat flour, grown right on the farm. Everybody grew enough for themselves. There was no particular sale. We would grow a little bit of wheat every year, enough to make our bread.   [CB]
Mother always had a few vines of hops for to make yeast.   [FT]

The valley lacked the climate for wheat growing, although they seemed reluctant to give up trying. But they were second to none in their efforts to improve their livestock and other crops, and in 1873 they formed the Chilliwack Agricultural Society, which included the settlers of Upper Sumas at the head of Sumas Lake. This led the following year to the first exhibition, or fall fair, and every year it was held in somebody's large barn, until Isaac Kipp gave the society a piece of land on which they put a building of their own.

So, in spite of a very limited market and very little money to spare, they were moving forward on several fronts, learning how to organize themselves, how to develop social institutions: churches, schools, a municipality, local courts of justice, with prominent citizens like David Miller and A. C. Wells as JPs. And yet their daily life remained simple, even what we might call primitive. They managed to have a resident minister, but there was no doctor nearer than Hope, no professional nurse, even. Some of them might own books about first aid and family medicine, on how to deal with fevers and broken bones and limbs that were out of joint, and a few people like A. C. Wells and Mary Kipp, would have acquired considerable experience in such things and could therefore handle emergencies. And that would have to do, unless a doctor somehow turned up on foot, by boat or on horseback—or the ill person was sent down to New Westminster on the steamer. Wells was also the local "dentist."

He had a set of forceps that he would use to extract teeth for people. Of course you had to brace yourself. There was no anaesthetic or anything at all; you had to take it as he'd give it to you.   [JK]
I was born in 1891, and we had no doctor. I was carrying trees into Mrs. Isaac Kipp's once, and she said, "You're a different looking guy than when I first saw you."
I says, "Why? When did you see me first?"
"Well," she says, "I brought you to this earth. And Mrs. Cupps, a half-breed lady, was the nurse."   [JH]
As a matter-of-fact, there'd be a call anytime during the night, and my mother used to get up and go to any place in the community. She more-or-less was the main nurse of the community when there was a sickness.   [CB]

When disasters came—a severe accident, a lost child, a house or barn burnt down—as in all pioneer communities, it was an occasion for the whole neighbourhood to rally around.

When I was about eleven years old, attending school at Camp Slough not far from Rosedale, there was a knock at the door. Of course we always gazed through the window as soon as we heard a knock, and there was a team of horses tied at the fence. The teacher went out, and when he came in he was looking very very serious. He said, "The Ryder children may go home now. Get your things at once and go home." And he didn't say anything else, as far as I remember. We all jumped up and went and got our coats on and everything. When we got out on the road we saw this smoke. The twins, who were four years younger than I, and were always great on running—they were quite athletic, and I never could run very fast—started out ahead of me and an older sister. And they ran all the way home; that would be close to two miles.

It was in the month of March, and the cold March wind was just howling. When I got there my youngest two sisters were sitting on boxes out in the front yard; and the few things that had been saved had been carried out into the yard, and nothing from the upstairs had been saved. We hadn't a big chimney, just a stove pipe running through the house; and sparks had got into the dry moss of the shakes or shingles or whatever it was. It was only when a neighbour saw this, and when my father and mother heard the crackle and the roar, that they realized that the house was all on fire. I suppose that sort of thing does stay with you more clearly than anything else, especially when my little sister said, "And everything is burnt, and our Sunday clothes are burnt, and our Sunday shoes are burnt, and you'll never believe it, but my best doll is burnt." So it was a real calamity to us children. Of course, few people kept any insurance in those days. We had none.

But there was a happy ending to the fire story, because before we Ryders knew what was happening, there were four or five men of the neighbourhood out, calling on other neighbours. And some gave hay—my father was short of hay that spring—some gave money, some gave furniture. Some said, "Well, you'll want to build again. We'll come and help build another house." And so, through the kindness of the neighbours—and this was quite typical of every part of the valley where a family had a disaster of that kind—the neighbours all came, regardless of religion or politics or anything. They just came because they were neighbours and wanted to help. And so we really had a better house, a frame house, than this old house that burned down.   [NP]

At 7 o'clock he'd blow his whistle

Until the CPR started operations, the riverboats ran between New Westminster and Yale. In the gold rush days there had been no particular schedule, but by the 1870s boats were running twice a week. As sternwheelers, with a shallow draught, they could land almost anywhere. They'd push their noses into the bank and run out a gangplank to load or unload passengers and cargo, or to take on cordwood for their boilers. The Chilliwack area's first landing place was at the mouth of the Chilliwack River, from whence most of the passengers would have had to disperse by canoe. But Messrs. Reece and Kipp found a spot on Shefford Slough more convenient for their own farms, and that's what became known as Chilliwack Landing, or simply "the Landing," and in time it acquired a wharf. Actually there came to be two landings, depending on the state of the river.

The upper landing was when the water was high. That's about two miles out of Chilliwack, the Beaver Landing they called it. The lower landing was about two miles further down.   [CB]

They used to call me "Steamboat Jack." I was always there to pull the rope in— up till I was eight years old, when we moved up here. It's a wonder I didn't go into the river. The boat used to whistle at half past six in the morning, and the next whistle would be at seven. And the farmers would be in there with their teams and wagons, and some on horseback, and one thing and another. The old captain, he'd never give them any warning at all. At seven o'clock he'd blow his whistle. You know the way the farmers are; they'd be all talking together, and away the horses would go—just like the Calgary Stampede. There'd be fellows running for horses, and horses rearing up in the buggies. Teams would get away sometimes. You'd see somebody on horseback a-ripping up the road after this team to head them off and get them stopped away up there someplace. It was quite a show when that old whistle would blow. And the farmers would do it time and time again. They'd never think about the whistle blowing. You know the way farmers are.

The boat was just a stern-wheeler. The old *Beaver* and the *Gladys* and *Ramona*, three of them used to come up there—different companies. It used to take all day to go down river. They'd sometimes get down there early, stay in Westminster all night, then come back the next day. Of course, they'd land at every little place along the river: Mission and Haney and Hammond, all all these little places. They wasn't named, some of them. You'd see a farmer out there with a calf, have a flag up or something. Down there at Sumas there was a big rock where they used to land.

There was the Chadseys and the Wilsons; they used to shoot ducks and grouse, and fetch them down and sell them to the steward on the boat. I think they got about 12½¢ apiece. Oh, the boat would be all lined up with grouse and ducks and one thing and another—take them down to Vancouver or Westminster and sell them.

My father used to buy produce and go down there, and I'd go down with him. We used to have wonderful meals on that boat—roast beef and potatoes and vegetables, and wonderful rhubarb pie—50¢. It was always 50¢, all you could eat. They had a bar on there. They used to get drinks for about 25¢. There was prohibition around here—that was a local regulation. The farmers used to come down and wait for the boat to come in. They wasn't supposed to sell when they were landed, just when they were going. But you know the way they do.   [JH]

The lower landing at the foot of Wellington St., Chilliwack (PABC 43261).

Wares in a trunk

It was the enterprising David Miller who started the first store in the valley. This would be around 1865, and it served the people of Sumas and Atchelitz. Twelve years later he had prospered enough to be able to build a large stone house on the little hill to the west of his landing. It was quite a landmark, until it was destroyed by fire.

Incidentally, his stonecutter and mason was a rather interesting fellow, a local farmer by the name of William Hall, who would probably have had a title if his father had not been disinherited by his aristocratic grandfather for "marrying beneath him," as they used to say. He came to the country as a corporal in the Royal Engineers, and like Matthew Hall (these Halls were not related), and Sergeant McColl, chose the valley for his military land grant. During the Crimean War he had been detailed to assist Florence Nightingale.

> He built a Dutch oven to facilitate the work of Florence Nightingale, so that she could heat water to sterilize the utensils that she used. He was a stonecutter by trade and a stonemason, and had worked, of course, on the Cariboo Road. He was the head stonecutter to build the penitentiary at New Westminster—that's the original penitentiary. And he built a stone marker on the international boundary line at Point Roberts. After his discharge from the Royal Engineers he was the toll-keeper at Yale for about two years. But he felt that there was not much chance of advancement in that field, so he took advantage of the offer from the Queen to take up a crown grant.   [FZ]

Chilliwack Landing had a store almost as early as Miller's Landing, and several people were involved in it at one time or another. But not till the Ashwells came did anything of consequence take root. Horatio Webb must have had something to do with this. As we know, he was Sarah Ashwell's brother, and they were all English people from Bedfordshire. Perhaps the hardware and furniture business in New Westminster wasn't doing so well in those difficult times. Whatever it was, George Ashwell must have decided that the grass looked greener in the Chilliwack Valley. So, in 1871, he bought a small parcel of land just north of Henry Kipp's. Whether he intended to farm it is not certain, but it wasn't long before he had started another store "with a few pieces of hardware in an unfurnished room of his house." said Mary Kipp, "while his wife displayed her wares in a trunk." As usual, Jim Kipp's account is more lively.

> Mrs. Ashwell was up visiting my mother, they were our next door neighbours and the only one she had to talk to, and she was talking about getting some things that women needed like threads and needles and prints, and something to make clothes with. If they wanted some yarn to darn something with they had to go to Westminster to get it. She said she thought that would be a splended idea to have that. Well, she went down to Westminster with two suitcases, I don't suppose they had suitcases in those days, but just some sort of container, and she saw all these things that she thought they would be needing, and brought them up here. As soon as these Chadseys and the rest of them around here, the Indians and the whole works, found out, they'd come and start a-buying. They found a store, a real store, right in the midst of them. She she kept adding more and more. She got into a trunk full, and she got six or eight trunks. Ashwell woke up then, and he thought, "Well, my land! If you can do so much business, I can do something too. So he went into the hardware and got his nails and saws and hammers and all this business. And pretty soon there was no room for them in the house, so they moved out of there and went down to Steamboat Landing.   [JK]

They bought one of the two little stores already there, and when the other one went out of business, theirs was the only one for a time. "So they charged pretty near what they liked," said Jim.

He'd give you credit, and first thing you'd know you'd have a great big bill, and you'd let it run, say for four months. And then after a while, "Lookit here, you bill's getting pretty big: I gotta have some settlement here. We can't let this go on forever." And, well, you didn't have any money, couldn't pay it; then he'd take a mortgage. He had lots of money, and he'd lend you the money to go on and navigate with. And, by golly, the first thing you'd know, old Ashwell owned nine different homesteads here. He had them corralled.   [JK]

By 1880 Ashwell and Miller were among the wealthiest men in the valley.

D. W. Miller residence (PABC 10388).

Red shirt Bill

Their stores were also the post offices. The first post office serving the Chilliwack area was at Codsville Landing on Nicomen Island; later it was moved to John McCutcheon's farm. Later still it was taken over by Mrs. Jane McDonald, who had a store at the landing.

"We could see her through the wicket
Take a stamp and gently lick it,
   Then place it upside down upon
      the mail" [Evans; 5].

Mail days were great occasions for people to meet and gossip as they stood or sat around waiting for the mail to be sorted. Letters were their only link with the family and friends they'd left behind. The newspapers were their windows to the outside world, then, as now, the world of politics, wars and other disasters. When someone was unable to pick up mail for himself, a neighbour would likely do it for him, then send it round with one of the children. But for many years the Atchelitz and Sardis district had its own rural delivery.

> Mr. Miller, the postmaster at Sumas, would put all our mail in a sack and give it to an Indian we had engaged, who would go from house to house, each party picking out their own mail. We paid him so much a year. He [the Indian] was the father-in-law of Billy Ballou, the mail carrier of the famous days in the gold rush.   [HW-1]

Billy Ballou was the first. He carried the mail on his back from the head of navigation to the Cariboo mines, and presumably all the way from New Westminster in the winter time. Then Frank Barnard took over, and the moment the Cariboo Road was passable he was running a stage line, meeting the boats at Yale and taking passengers, mail and express on into the interior. Barnard's Express Company had the mail contract for years, and when the steamboats couldn't run, he had to engage a carrier to bring both mail and express, and passengers, too, if there were any, up from New Westminster any way he could. The man who had the job for many years was a relic of the gold rush days was a memorable character by the name of Bill Bristol. Some of the valley people drove team for him when the mail had to go by land, from post to post, men like Reuben Nowell, Henry Kipp and Horatio Webb. Bristol lived on what came to be known as Bristol Island, a few miles down river from Hope; and in his later years he was a good friend of young Martin Starret, who grew up on a stump ranch just across a slough from Bristol's farm.

> He was probably in his late 60s in the early '90s when I first remember seeing him. Being a neighbour of mine, living only half a mile or so away, I saw quite a bit of him. He was a typical eastern Yank. He spoke with a drawl. He was a loud mouth, and profane. I know a lot of these profane men that are whirlwinds, and he was one. He wasn't an overly large man at all; I suppose he'd stand five foot ten. And he was barrel chested and had a rather hooked nose and a very kindly eye, and was very jocular in his manner, unless he was perplexed. I never knew him to panic.
> He left his hair generally long, and he had a beard. He'd trim it once in a while. He wore a slouch hat and he never tried to be neat. He'd have overalls, and he wouldn't have any suspenders as a rule. He wouldn't know where he'd left his belt; he'd have it tied with bailing rope. He never worried what people thought of him. What he wanted was results. But there was nothing exceptional about what he could do as far as his strength was concerned. It was the stamina that counted with him, his remarkable "stay-with-it". In after years he walked from Princeton right over to Hope in a day. My father told me any gait he'd start out with in the morning, why, he'd keep that up till long after dark. As my father expressed it, "It would tire any other man to walk with him, just see-saw, see-saw all day long."
> This Bill Bristol, he was born in Syracuse, New York, and he'd come around the Horn in a windjammer. He got off at San Francisco, or 'Frisco as he used to call it; and he worked in the mines there in '49. He must have hung around there quite a while, because he came up here in 1858, and as far as I know he didn't get any further than I guess, it was, Sailor Bar or American Bar above Hope here.
> At that time, like after the Cariboo Road was completed to Barkerville from Yale, he got the job from the Barnard Express for carrying mail and express between Westminster and Yale. It was only in the season when the boats wouldn't run, like in the fall and early spring—all winter too, of course, when the water was shallow. A steamboat drawing 18 inches of water and very often unable to make it over these riffles, and when that happened Mr. Bristol would have to carry the mail.
> When the weather was good in the early fall he'd use a rowboat. Then when the winter came he'd use nothing but a dugout cedar canoe with a shovel nose to go over the ice. There was ice running in the water—icebergs. Maybe some of them would be 20 feet across, and maybe six inches to a foot thick. Well, he'd get the old canoe on top of some of them, and then he'd back up and get in between them, and push around with poles and paddles. He had to line it outside with sheet metal or tin, so as the ice wouldn't cut the canoe. It was just an ordinary, Indian built, shovel-nosed canoe. I suppose it would be two feet to two and a half feet wide, and maybe five fathoms long; that would be 30 feet. And there were thwarts, of course, in it; they weren't seats.

BARNARD'S
Express Line Stages
CARRYING H. M. MAILS,

Will make

Regular Weekly Trips from Barkerville,

Arriving in Yale on Thursdays, in time to connect with the steamer "Onward" for New Westminster, and with the H. B. Co.'s steamer "Enterprise,"

ARRIVING IN VICTORIA ON SATURDAYS.

The California steamers leave Victoria on the 7th and 22d of each month.

ap27 3m   F. J. BARNARD.

Bill Bristrol (PABC 5018).

They were there to keep it wide, and sometimes they were just little round poles. Well, the first thing a passenger would do he would want to sit on them, and then Mr. Bristol would have to explain to them, "You sit on the bottom. You sit right down there on your behinder and stay there!" He said the passengers often objected to the rough food they were eating. Mr. Bristol's mainstay was dried salmon. Granny Rabbit said one dried salmon would last him six days.

He employed nothing but an Indian crew to work with him, as he could, I suppose, not exactly bully them, but encourage them to a greater extent than he could any white people he might employ. Another thing, an Indian wasn't afraid to jump out into the water and wade, and if it was shallow, he didn't object to getting his feet wet. When it came to paddling, the Indian, having wielded a paddle for years and years, first on one side of a canoe and then on the other, the left was almost the same as the right. In guiding these craft up stream there was no such thing as feathering it or hitching it at the stern in order to direct the craft on its course. From the time he left Westminster to Yale, every motion was to propel it ahead, as time seemed to be a principal element.

He told me that going downstream was the most tiresome. "You're practically in one position all the time," he said. "Paddle, paddle, paddle, one side and then the other side." Sometimes we would use a boat, and long before we got down to New Westminster I could just imagine I was sitting on pins and needles.

"When I landed there I'd always grab my paddle, because somebody might pick it up and use it. So I'd carry the paddle with me and the locksack. I was known down there as Red Shirt Bill."

Well, the way it was told me by a gentleman named Bob Hume, Bill Bristol, in stepping out of the canoe after he landed, would never let go of the paddle. He'd carry it up town with his mail sacks on one shoulder. He said he'd have the paddle as protection against the Indian dogs that would come to bite him. He looked so queer coming up the beach in this red shirt and hunched over with those mail packs, they all wanted to bite him.

He told me that during the last few years of carrying the mail this Old Yale Road was built, and he was able to drive a team from Yale to Westminster. But before that it was all river work.   [MS]

Raish Webb was involved in at least one of these land journeys. It was during the winter of 1882; Bill Bristol left New Westminster by steamer with the mail bags, as usual on a Thursday morning. But a cold wind got up, and by the time they were opposite Fort Langley, the river was frozen so hard they had to tie up to the bank. Not till Saturday was the ice actually hard enough for Bill to cross to the fort with the mail bags and a passenger, a Mr. Green, who was going up to work on the CPR survey above Yale.

> On arrival at Langley the only team they could get was an ox team, with which he went as far as Langley Prairie where he struck the trunk road to Hope; there he got a team of horses and sleigh from Innes brothers, who were large farmers; they took him as far as Mr. York's, Upper Sumas, where he secured another team and sleigh, just stopping long enough to eat. He telegraphed me to meet him with the team and sleigh at Chilliwack at 6 p.m.; I did so, for there was big pay at this work. The last team he used were not shod and the horses got footsore coming around Sumas Lake which made him two hours late. I took the Chilliwack mail down to the post office at the Landing, whilst Bristol and Green ate their suppers. About 9 p.m. we started for Hope, with nearly a foot of snow on the ground; Henry Kipp had gone to Hope that morning with his team and sleigh to meet the down-coming mail from the upper country, in response to a telegram he had received from Bonner's [Barnard's] Express at Yale. More snow fell after Mr. Kipp left, so there was no track left.
>
> We got to Popkum about 11 o'clock. Waking up Mr. and Mrs. William Knight we unhitched our horses and fed them. Mrs. Knight, like her dear mother, soon prepared our supper with a smile. We stopped until a little after midnight to give our horses a rest. [HW-1]
>
> The next 12 miles, to Jones' place on the Ohamil reserve, took them nearly eight hours. The first big obstacle was a bridge, which had been cleared of snow by the wind; but no sooner had the three of them pushed and dragged the runners over that, than the sleigh sank through the snow into a deep rut and turned over. So everything had to be unlashed and unloaded, and expecting the rut continued up the steep slope ahead of them, they, and the passenger, too, toted the sacks of mail and express up to the top of the hill.
>
> After loading at the top of the hill we started off feeling sure our worst trouble was over as we had about four miles of heavy timber to pass through, but our troubles were waiting us. A large fir tree had fallen across the road from the side of the mountain; we had to unload everything, putting it over the tree, take our horses off, lift the sleigh over, then separate our horses and take them around the root end of the tree. In less than four miles we did this five times, we got to Jones about 8 a.m. All we had to give us light was a candle. We all enjoyed breakfast. Mrs. Jones was of Indian blood but had been educated in a school where she was taught cooking; her house was always very clean. We stopped there about two hours, then started for Hope. By the time we got half way to Hope we met the mail coming down with Mr. Kipp. Mr. S. Tingley of the Bonner's [Barnard's] Express was with him. Bristol went back with them, Mr. Green and myself going on to Hope where there was a man awaiting to take it on to Yale. Mr. Green told me afterwards that they charged him $40 for that trip. [HW-1]

When the trains started running Bill Bristol retired to his island, and Barnard's Express gave him a gold watch, "in remembrance of his long and faithful service." But whenever the trains were delayed by slides and washouts, as happened quite frequently to begin with, people would realize how much they missed the old chap who had brought them their mail so regularly, whatever the weather. By then he had other things to do, like clearing his land and farming it, and walking great distances over mountain trails. He died in the early winter of 1909, retaining to the end his dry sense of humour.

> "Wa-a-all, doctor," said this inveterate traveller, "I think I'll be goin' on a lo-o-ong trip today."

NEW OPPORTUNITIES

He called it Centreville

On May 15th, 1880, a blast of dynamite at Yale announced to the echoing hills that the CPR had begun to carve out its right of way through the Fraser Canyon. It's even possible that the sound reverberated into the Chilliwack Valley. Certainly, the settlers there had known for some time that a railway was going to be built on the other side of the river. Already the optimism of the days of the gold fields was creeping back, and the old market for meat, fodder and dairy products was about to be revived.

One of the minor consequences was that the Landing got a new store, financed by none other than Captain John Irving, one of the famous coastal captains. By 1890 he controlled the Canadian Pacific Navigation Co. and, with the *Reliance* and the splendid new *William Irving*, Irving had already collared the lion's share of the river traffic. His working partner was a young man who had immigrated with wife and family a few years before: John Calvin Henderson, a son of A. C. Henderson of Rosedale.

> My grandfather came here first, and he wrote back to my father in Kansas, and him and his wife and son, Arthur, came. He worked at the logging camp up at Popkum. Then Captain Irving set him up in business down at the Landing here at Chilliwack, just when the CPR was going through, you see. The boats all came up from New Westminster and landed right at his store. It was a general store—overalls and nails and groceries.   [JH]
>
> "He proved a good man for the valley," said Mary Kipp, "hunting up a market for our produce and converting it into cash, so we felt a peculiar sensation at having some money in our pockets, which before this had been hard to get, our friends in New Westminster preferring to buy from our American cousins" [*Progress*; 25 June 1958].

1880 was also the year Mrs. Matilda Harrison bought a little house at the Landing from an Indian, and had it remodeled, and started serving meals to people who were waiting for the boat. She was a sister of the Ryder brothers—John and the twins, Cory and Jim—a widow with a small child, who had come out from Ontario two years before, hoping to be able to start a new life in the west.

> She had three brothers out here, so she felt that she had somebody to come to; and they helped her for a while. But she wanted to be self-supporting. So she was advised by this Mrs. Ashwell, the wife of this man who had a little store down at the Landing, to open up a boarding house. She said, "You're trying to walk these rough roads, and your little boy with you, and sell books. Mrs. Harrison, you'll *never* make a living selling books to people in Chilliwack now, because the little bit of money they have they need for provisions and perhaps to hire some help to clear the land." So Mrs. Harrison took this tip and, I guess, received a little help. And they had this first hotel put up, called the Valley Hotel, quite a humble little place. She said Mrs. Ashwell was like a sister to her. "If you haven't enough room to put people up, I have some extra bedrooms, and you turn them over to me. They'll pay you, not me. We're making a good living from these people through our little store."   [NP]

Mrs. Harrison had considerable ability, and her venture flourished. She and J. C. Henderson managed to start up at a propitious time, when railway construction was stirring up the whole Fraser Valley, it was an opportune time to open a store or boarding house. Jack Henderson mentioned that his father "used to hire an Indian to take supplies—that's groceries, overalls, nails and stuff like that—across to the employees" who were building the railroad.

But, busy as it was, the Landing could not accommodate any expansion. Not only was it hemmed in by an Indian reserve, but what there was of it was being rapidly eroded by the river. So the focus began to shift to a point two miles inland where the Landing road joined the main thoroughfare, the Yale Road. This was precisely at the boundary between Isaac Kipp's farm and Reuben Nowell's, and running south along this boundary was another road leading to the farm of Charles Young. When the trains started running the Young Road was extended northward to a ferry landing, opposite the CPR's station at the mouth of the Harrison River. So there developed Five Corners, a natural place to start a village particularly when Isaac Kipp in 1881 laid out a townsite on his land immediately west of the corners. He called it Centreville. This was appropriate enough for it was also the name of his hometown back in Brant County, Ontario. Centreville, Ontario was a tiny place, and still is, though today it goes by another name. But Centreville, B.C. had already acquired an Anglican church, a blacksmith's shop, and a school not far away. Within a few years it also acquired a grist mill (moved over from Miller's Landing), a carriage builder's shop, an inn, a small general store, a county court house, a Methodist church and the valley's first residential doctor.

Mr. and Mrs. John Ryder; Albert standing, Mary, Florence and Maggie, and Stanley on his father's knee; Cheam (PABC 43210).

Dr. John Cotter Henderson—not to be confused with his first cousin at the Landing, John Calvin Henderson—was one of the first to arrive on the new transcontinental trains. He had trained at the University of Glasgow Medical School. It's Nellie Patsquin—who knew him well—who said, "He had just received his medical degree at Glasgow University when he came out."

> He, of course, found, that there was no hospital, no other doctor. There had been one for a very short period, and his field of labour would be from Hope to Mission on both sides of the river. The roads when he came were very rough; some of them were mere trails, and so he would have to go on foot to many a lonely settler's cabin to attend a sick person. If an Indian came over, or a settler from the other side of the river with a message of somebody sick, somebody had had an accident, he would have to get to the river as quickly as he could. He knew the places where Indians would take you across in a canoe.
>
> Two or three years after he came he married a Miss Fanny McCutcheon. Mr. John McCutcheon, her father, had the first telegraph office. Mrs. Henderson was a true doctor's wife. She would keep the fires burning and always be ready when he came in to see that he was made comfortable, and help him all she could at any hour of the day or night. Sometimes, as his wife told later, he would come back from visiting a patient at Popkum or at Hope, and when he'd get home soaking wet and tired, there'd be a man knocking at the door. "There's a women expecting a baby, and she's in a terrible way. You'll just have to come right away quick." Dr. Henderson never refused a call to duty. He would get into dry clothes immediately. Mrs. Henderson would give him a cup of hot tea and a bite to eat, and he would saddle a fresh mount and be off with the messenger as fast as he could. They would go down to the river some place where an Indian would take them across, and there'd be horses probably on the other side. It could be way on in the morning by the time he got back.
>
> He was very persevering, very professional in his manner, and very meticulous about his personal appearance; and the people had almost a reverence for Dr. Henderson when he came into the home. He was kindness itself and gentleness itself, and yet he never dilly-dallied with jokes and that, to the extent that they lost their regard for him. They had a feeling for Dr. Henderson that I've never heard them speak of in the same terms of anybody else.
>
> Dr. Henderson had a great respect for those early pioneer women who had walked miles, sometimes, to assist him at childbirth, and at other times.
>
> His operating table was the kitchen table or a long narrow table in his office. There was no other doctor to give an anaesthetic, and so Mr. Harry Barber would administer it in minor cases. In major cases the man was usually taken to New Westminster, or a doctor was sent up by boat. And, of course, this took time, and the patient in the meantime might die. Conditions were very crude at that time.   [NP]

If a tooth was bothering someone, A. C. Wells' forceps seem to have been the only recourse—until the days of the travelling dentists.

> Dr. Hacking, I think from New Westminster, used to come up here. I don't know whether he was the first one or not, but he used to go to Henderson's to do his extracting. He got me in there one day. I had six or eight to take out. [My] teeth were very chalky and they didn't last very long. They got me on one of these chairs, spread out flat. His office chair was a collapsible affair; you could spread it out like a table. And they had me spread out on this thing, and Henderson was giving me the anaesthetic, chloroform, to get me to sleep. And he got me till I was just going off—didn't know where I was, whether in this world or the next one; and this fool thing collapsed, and my feet flew up straddle my neck, and I went down in a pile and rolled off onto the floor. Away went the chloroform and everything else. I was so scared I thought they was trying to kill me. I was only a youngster at the time.   [JK]

We hadn't the money to go home

In 1887 the CPR brought in the Mellard family. Samuel Mellard had been the manager of the leading hardware store in Bedford, England, and his wife Kate was a sister of Horatio Webb and Sarah Ashwell. The Ashwells had been on a trip back home, leaving Raish Webb to look after their store. While they were there, like proper British Columbians, they'd been telling the Mellards about the beautiful Chilliwack Valley, and what splendid opportunities there would be for a man like Sam, till Sam had become

just a little bit crazy in his blood to come out to a foreign country. My husband, you see, was a hardware man and had a good position, and he just took it in his head to come back with my sister and her husband. Of course, I refused at once. I wouldn't come, I said. I had my mother there, and I had three little girls. Some of the younger people said, "What in the world are you going to that god-forsaken country for? British Columbia! Out of the world nearly!" Then I thought, "Well, if I don't go, and he happens to lose that job where he is, he'll say, 'Well, I could have had a chance to go to British Columbia'." So I thought, "I'll stand it for a little while, anyway."

"Interior of a colonial sleeping-car" on the CPR (from the *Illustrated London News*, Dec. 15, 1888).

We came on the CPR; that was about the second or third trip, I think, it had gone through. It was the year of Queen Victoria's Jubilee. We got off the train at Harrison Station, and we had to walk down, and there was the river, the Fraser, and a man who would take the mail. [KM]

One pictures this apprehensive young Englishwoman, with her husband and three small children, stepping off the train on to a platform in the middle of nowhere, mountains all around, and directly in front a broad swiftly flowing river that could only be crossed in a dugout canoe paddled by an Indian. On the other side they would have been put in a wagon or a buggy and driven along a rutty road across the marginal meadows or through patches of scrub, and still there would seem to be nothing there—"nothing at all!" she said. "Just fields and farm places, a clump of trees here and there." As she passed the Corners she would have noticed a scattering of wooden houses and unpainted sheds, and a tiny wooden church. Down at the Landing, where her sister lived, there would have been an even smaller clump of buildings: two stores, a boarding house and a shed or two. And as if all that wasn't wild and woolly enough, a few nights after their arrival a farmer up the road held a wedding party for one of his daughters, which was followed by a shivaree.

> When this thing started we were in bed, and I heard this noise, and of course it frightened me. These people were shooting off guns, and they had whistles. We could hear them at the Landing. I jumped out of bed, and my sister said, "Oh, what's the matter? Are you sick?" I said, "No. But, Sarah," I said, "we'll all be killed!" And she said, "Why? What?" I said, "There's an awful noise outside." I remember how frightened I was. I thought there was a whole host of Indians had come down, because where my sister and her husband lived it was the Indian reservation, and we were right at the water's edge, you see. "Aw," she says, "I'll tell you about it in the morning. You get to bed," she says, "you won't hear that in a little while." So I went to bed. And when they were at breakfast table they were roaring, her husband and her, at me thinking it was such a terrible thing.
>
> It wasn't many days after we'd come here before my husband was homesick—nothing to do, you see, nothing in his line, like. My brother had the farm, but my husband was just an office man. And I said, "Don't you think you're smart, coming out here from a good position." [KM]

But it wasn't long before this town-mouse found a place for himself in this very rural community. The post office had recently been moved up to Centreville from the Ashwell store, and the new postmaster, Samuel Cawley, an elderly Englishman, was having to retire because of ill health.

> Raish said one day, "Say! I believe I could get Sam a job." And he talked to the people, and he said, "I have a brother-in-law that's doing nothing. He's well educated. Perhaps he'll take the job." Of course, he wasn't used to post office work, but then he *was* well educated and could take anything on like that. And he took it—$16 a month.
>
> But when I came out here I thought three weeks would do me. I used to cry every day for about four years to go home. Then I came to the conclusion that it was no good; we hadn't the money to go home. And from then onwards I was very content. I've been here now well on to 75 years, and I've been to Vancouver not 12 times. [KM]

When she told me these things Kate Mellard was 101, a frail little woman, but still mentally active and spry. From where she was living she could look right down on the Five Corners that had seemed so insignificant when she first made their acquaintance. Yet even at that time a great deal was already beginning to happen. The muddy Yale Road that intersected the village was every year becoming a more viable means of communication. The coming of the railway was helping to shift the emphasis from the Landing, even though one had to cross a river to get to it. By 1888, Ashwell and Henderson, the friendly rivals, had both moved their stores to the new centre of business. Henderson had bought out his partner, Captain John Irving, and teamed up with his brother, Hunter Henderson, and together they had built a new store right on one of the corners, with a public meeting hall for a second storey. Only the little Valley Hotel remained at the Landing, but not for long. The Corners already had an inn of sorts that called itself the Bartlett House, but it was not likely to compete with anything that Martha Harrison had in mind.

Noted for its excellent butter

Behind all this clustering at the Five Corners was the growing prosperity of the farmers, and the new markets that were opening up to them, first in the construction camps, and then in the rapidly growing cities at the coast. Of course, the merchants down there continued to import a great deal of farm produce from across the border, which disgusted the valley people, and may well have been one of the reasons for their continued efforts to improve their crops and their stock whenever possible. A. C. Wells, for instance, availed himself of the newly completed railway to travel back to Ontario and purchase quality livestock, including some Durham bulls. Already, in 1885, he had built the valley's first creamery and brought in an expert butter and cheese maker from Ontario to run it, and for a time it was the only cheese factory in the province. Later on, the Edenbank Creamery, as it was called, became British Columbia's first cooperative. Another first for western Canada happened when Wells built the first upright silo in 1891.

Around the Creamery and this busy, progressive farm grew the village of Sardis. The name had been picked at random from a Bible by Adam Vedder's wife. They were neighbours of A. C. Wells and so was Horatio Webb, who had settled there in 1878. Some ten years later Sardis became the site of the Methodist home for Indian children: this grew into the Coqualeetza Residential School and provided an education for children from the Methodist missions on the coast.

All through these years the Chilliwack Agricultural Association with its annual fall fairs was a source of advice and encouragement, so, too, was the Dominion Experimental Farm, which came into being in 1888 across the river at Agassiz. Nevertheless, it took some time for farming to settle down into the things the valley grew best, given the soil and climate. There was a prolonged effort, for instance, to plant orchards, and fruit was even shipped by train to the prairies. But, after the turn of the century, it became too difficult to compete with the Okanagan orchards and their superior growing conditions, so the valley people began to concentrate more on hay and oats, root vegetables, particularly potatoes, beef cattle and dairy cattle.

Almost from the beginning some of them were making butter and sending it up into the Cariboo and other mining areas. Some twenty years later, a B.C. Directory for 1892 informs us Chilliwack was "noted for its excellent butter, which has a delicious flavour, and is made in large quantities."

First of all they used to send their butter to Victoria. I think it was in a hundred pound boxes. In later years they shipped it to New Westminster. And that was the only means that they had of getting any cash. They'd load it on to the wagon, and the boat left the dock down at the upper landing at seven o'clock in the morning. They'd take it down twice a week. That would be about ten miles from here.   [CB]

To make butter in those days we used to set the milk in pans. Some people had deep creamers that cooled it, then they'd drain the milk off at the bottom till they got down to where the cream would show in a glass. But we had it set in pans in a very cool dairy that was built onto the log cabin. Mother would skim the cream off, and when it was ready for to churn, she put it in this wooden dash churn. I've sat in the corner, before I was ready to go to school, and churned butter many a day with one of these wooden dashes. The churn itself is like a small wooden barrel made of some hard wood, and the dash is a piece of wood like a cross, like an 'X', and it's nailed on the end of, you might say, a stick about the size of a broom handle. And you dash that up and down in the cream, you see, and keep it stirred up until it turns to butter. Then Mother would make that up at a nice butter table where she used a lovely roller, an octagon roller that I think my oldest brother must have made for her. She'd make this butter up into prints with a mold that will print out a pound of butter. You'd fill that mold right up with butter; and it had a plunger at the top, and you'd push down on that, and it would push that pound of butter out onto a table. And she would wrap it up in a piece of special paper—waxed, I guess it would be—that would make it air-proof; and of course it would keep in that for quite a long time. Then she would take it into Chilliwack and sell it to the stores for products. That was one of the ways we had of getting a livelihood. She could always sell all the butter she could make. Then the skim milk, of course, was fed to the calves and pigs.

We went from that to a little separator called an Alexandra Cream Separator. One could milk about as fast as that thing would separate it. Then the question was what to do with the cream. We're getting more cows all the time. So we shipped the cream by boat to New Westminster to a creamery in a big barrel that had a tin lining in it. We would ship it there when it had pretty well filled up, because it was made into butter and didn't need to be sweet, as long as it was stirred up and kept in a cool place so that it didn't go bad in any way. These cans had a heavy lid on them and a padlock put on it; and we had a key and they had a key down there at the dairy. It would be taken to the riverboat and to New Westminster in one day, and the next day it would come back empty. And that's the way we did for quite a while.

In the early days you just milked in the summer. We didn't milk in the winter time because you couldn't handle the by-product so well as you could in the summer. So you'd have the cows freshening about April, and then dry them up again in October, and just keep one cow milking throughout the wintertime for our own use.

Mother was great for making Devonshire cream. That is made by placing a pan of milk—when the cream is all up to the top after its been setting for say 24 or 36 hours—on the back of the stove, and let it set there until just before it comes to a boil. And when you'd see that the cream was all wrinkled and sort of moving, twitching like there were nerves in it, she would know it was ready. Then she'd set it in a cool place until it got perfectly cold and this cream would be solid, and you could just scoop it off. And it was the most delightful tasting thing I ever tasted.   [FT]

He lived in a hollow stump

Obviously, by the end of the 1880s some of the farms were becoming well established. Jack McCutcheon remembered the Isaac Kipp place as

> a sort of little community of itself. To begin with there was a large family, and always a lot of hired men around, together with other company. It was a no uncommon sight to see from 12 to 20 people sit down to a meal at that great huge kitchen at Ike Kipp's.   [JM]

At the same time, there were homesteads that were just being opened up, particularly in the area known as East Chilliwack, over towards the mountains. Without question, it was the wettest part of the whole valley, riddled with springs and heavily forested, except for a boggy clearing known as the Little Prairie. A young homesteader, like Joseph Brannick, must have wondered sometimes what on earth he was doing there.

As a matter of fact, until he got a shack built, he lived in a hollow stump, just about where this house is sitting now. Then they built a log house, quite a good sized house, all done by voluntary labour, or bees, as they called them. I was born in that house.

My father was brought up on a homestead on Owen Sound, and he left that country because it had too many rocks, and he'd heard about the wonderful West. At that time the CPR hadn't been all the way through, so he went down through Chicago, worked in Washington for part of the year, then came up to Victoria. When he landed here, in July 1882, he had only 50¢ in his pocket.

Most of the land in this part of the country had been homesteaded at that time, and there were only one or two places left. But it's a very fertile part of the valley, and while I don't know of any area on the flat that isn't very fertile, each has it's own problems. The problem here is seepage from the mountain. This area here isn't any good unless it is under drained. There were a great many beaver in the country at that time, and he'd just get a beaver house or a beaver dam out, and about two days afterwards the country would be flooded again—that on top of the very heavy timber—big heavy cedar. We didn't have one Douglas fir on the farm, and right close to us there was all kinds of Douglas fir. And you have a lot of underground log problems here. What had happened was that the streams and floods and everything brought in logs, and then these mountain streams would overflow and cover these logs with silt. We'd have a crop of trees on top, and a crop of logs underground.

They'd clear a piece of land—cut some timber off. But most of the good cedar was put on a burning pile and burned. If we had it today it would be worth a fortune pretty well. Most people used Chinese labour. After the CPR got finished many of the Chinese they brought out took to the land, and there were groups who would brush. You'd get a few acres brushed if you had enough money to pay for them. You'd pay them a dollar a day.   [CB]

There were a large number of Chinamen living in shacks on the farms, employed in clearing the land. For payment they had the use of the land for two or three years for growing potatoes. I don't know how we would have gotten the land cleared without them. They would work all winter, brushing, grubbing and burning, splitting rails and posts.   [JM]

So people would clear a piece of land—as much as they could—then they would seed it down. And they'd gradually get a few cows. Then the pasture was a problem. Some of them west of here had what they called the Big Prairie. That would be down on the Prairie Central area, and cattle used to run at large there, run through the bush. They were all belled, and everybody knew the other fellow's bell. They all seemed to have a different tone. The problem was to get a good bell cow. You'd get the odd cow that was very quiet and wouldn't ring the bell. But you'd pick the cow that you'd think was the best. And in those early days you could hear the bells for miles and miles in the country. Everybody'd get out in the evening and start to look for their cows. And the neighbours would say, "Well, I heard you bell over in that area." And that's the way it went on for a good many years. Then as time went on we had a few more cows.

The wild animals were quite bad, the bears particularly. Any time there was a pig squealing the neighbours from all around ran to that corner. I remember many a time they chased the bear off with an axe. They didn't have too many guns at that time.   [CB]

Nearly every farmer had a Chinaman employed. They would work for years on the same farms, sort of permanent fixtures, and reliable, too.   [JM]

We had a Chinese helper all the time—up till not far from the first war. They got something like $15 a month, or probably less than that in the wintertime. There was usually a winter wage and a summer wage. The Chinese always had a shack, and always ate in the kitchen. The Chinese don't like to eat at the same table as white people, or didn't at that time.   [CB]

Such enterprise, exhibited by a woman!

On April 16th, 1891, the valley acquired a newspaper, appropriately named the *Chilliwack Progress*. W. T. Jackman, a printer from Ontario, where small newspapers were altogether too plentiful, had been looking for a place where he could publish on his own. Perhaps he had already got wind of the valley's growing prosperity through one of its many contacts with eastern Canada. At any rate, he landed with his printing press in this little place that was becoming known as the town of Chilliwack, rather than the village of Centreville, and began to print and publish a paper of his own. As a result the valley people not only were better informed about the world at large, but could now see themselves reflected in items of local news, editorials and advertisements, all of which would make for more self-awareness and sophistication. No matter that two of the four pages were printed in Ontario, the other two set out to boost the local ego by making much of the economic upswing in both the province and the district. "We may look upon the length and breadth of this beautiful valley." proclaimed the printer-editor in the very first issue, "and say to the world as we lift the veil, 'Look upon the prettiest, richest and best spot on the earth!' "

The early issues give us some idea of the local boom that was underway, with new buildings under construction and new industries springing up weekly. "There is a daily increase in population." It is evident that real estate agents have gathered at the honey pot and are hard at work. Some 80 town lots are for sale "close to Mrs. Harrison's new hotel." There's a fruit cannery about to open; Sam Mellard, as well as being postmaster, has become a conveyancer and notary public, and G. R. Ashwell announces "All parties indebted to us are requested to settle up the amount of their accounts to Jan. 1, 1891, on or before 10th day of May, by cash or note" [*Progress*; 14 May 1891].

Tennis courts at the Harrison House, 1903 (PABC 43240).

The editor wraps himself in the robes of a prophet and predicts that a tramway will soon be running from the Landing to the town, that there will be a daily steamer to New Westminster, that Main Street will be graded and be given sidewalks, that the town will get some fire protection, and—most daring of all—that there will be a railway into the valley that very summer, extending from the branch line that the CPR had just completed between Mission and the U.S. border. Unfortunately in those days railway projects came and went all too easily; Chilliwack had to wait another 19 years before it got its own railway station.

Although the first homesteaders had arrived barely thirty years before, people were beginning to look back, as well as forward, realizing perhaps how much of the stability and prosperity of the valley was due to those same first settlers, most of whom were still in their prime: the Kipps, the Chadseys, Reece, Miller, Nowell, Wells, McCutcheon, Adam Vedder and others like them, to say nothing of their womenfolk. They and a handful of more recent arrivals were still the pillars of their respective communities, having proved themselves, either as farmers or merchants by their public spirit, their general integrity, and sheer hard work. The equally forward-looking editor of the *Chilliwack Progress* underlined it all in a series of short biographies; and one of them, rather surprisingly for those days, was a woman's [*Progress*; 21 May 1891].

Mrs. Harrison's enterprise had been growing with the times. We learn that she arrived in the province in 1878 "and two years afterwards built the Valley Hotel at the Landing and commenced in a small way to keep hotel." She soon had to enlarge her premises, and "a short time ago was obliged to build what is now known as the Harrison House.... Such enterprise, exhibited by a woman, is very commendable indeed."

From an earlier account we gather that this was one of "Chilliwack's grandest and most costly buildings." It faced on Wellington Street, the road that came up from the Landing, and was only a short distance from the Five Corners. The main part of the building measured 38 ft. by 50 ft., was two and a half storeys high, and there was a wing which included the kitchen. "The furnishings throughout," said the report, "are new and first class in every respect.... A beautiful balcony which is carried along the front of the building greets the eye on approaching and is a credit to the designer, as it adds greatly to the appearance of the building.... We bespeak for the House a wide patronage" [*Progress*; 14 May 1891].

> Every one of those bedrooms had wall-to-wall carpet—two floors anyway had carpet. There was the gents' parlour downstairs on the left as you entered, and the ladies' parlour on the right: a large dining room through an archway off the ladies' parlour, and a door leading into it from the hall. A sister of mine and two nieces helped in the dining room, so that the Harrison House was run pretty well as a family concern.

> Mrs. Harrison was a very gracious hostess; she always dressed very nicely and kept a very high class hotel. She never allowed a drop of liquor to be sold in the house. As the stage coach, as they called it, came up from the Landing to Centreville, it stopped with the guests for the Harrison House. When the boat came in you heard the whistle, and the next thing you knew along came these prancing horses; and they drew up at this platform, which had about four or five steps going down to the sidewalk, and the ladies gingerly picked up their skirts and stepped down, and the men tripped down and gave them their hand, and it was all very courtly. Mrs. Harrison never came out on the sidewalk, but she had the door open and stayed just inside and shook hands with her guests; and they registered and were assigned to their rooms.

> Quite a few notables were entertained at the Harrison Hotel: Earl Grey, Governor-General, was one of them, and judges from New Westminster, who would come up on court cases; and there were the old standbys, who stayed there all the time—old bachelors, and that. The commercial travellers would arrange their itineraries so they could spend their weekends at the Harrison House, because it was like going home, they said.

Mrs. Harrison had bought some land a little farther west, toward the Landing; and here she kept two jersey cows. She had part of this land planted in black currants, red currants and gooseberries—small fruits of that kind—and also in tree fruit, so that the table was a great drawing card. They had lovely jersey cream, and they had their own canned fruit. And they had their own pickles. I can remember as a child seeing these great pots of pickles. I'd go down to the kitchen where Jen, the Chinaman, presided—and he did preside. You had to be very careful when you stepped into the kitchen. He'd wave this great big carving knife at you, and you'd run. You didn't need to be told. But I still remember the smell of those luscious fruits and pickles and jams that were cooked in that kitchen. These travellers were so thrilled to sit down to a table where there was such beautiful home food.

The grounds were particularly noteworthy. Mrs. Harrison had an old man named Chapman, who was a very wonderful horticulturalist. Some said that he was a Norwegian; there was a slight accent there. He was very curt, almost rude, in his replies to questions about the garden. But his flower beds were beautiful, his flowering shrubs were beautiful; he had fuchsia trees high in big tubs. He kept the lawn just like velvet for lawn croquet and lawn tennis. That was one of the amusements of the guests. The dining room girls, of course, were just one of the family, and they would get through with their work and go out and play tennis, too.

People would ask Mrs. Harrison if they just might come in and walk around the grounds because they were so beautiful. People were clearing the land, and there just wasn't time to improve their ground, although a few people at Sumas and at Sardis did have nice flower gardens at this time—it would be the 1890s I'm speaking of. During the 1894 flood this beautiful lawn was covered with water, deep enough that young men who were boarding there went for canoe rides around the lawn. And that was one of the amusements!

Mrs. Harrison's brother, Jim Ryder, was a permanent resident. He was known as Uncle Jim not only to his nieces and nephews, but "the whole country over," said Mary Kipp, "as was proven by a wag, who made a bet that he could mail a letter up the coast addressed to 'Uncle Jim, B.C.' and he would receive it. This was done, and it reached Mr. Ryder in due time" [*Progress*; 25 June 1958].

Mrs. Harrison paid off all the mortgage on her hotel, and when she retired in 1907 she sold it and built a house for herself and Uncle Jim. "She is often seen on the street," wrote Mary Kipp, "giving help and advice to others, herself a landmark in the valley" [Ibid].

Planks over the ice

Her son, Jeff Harrison, was quite a character. He brought the mail over from Harrison to Chilliwack in a canoe for years and years. He was one of the best-hearted fellows that ever was. Everybody liked Jeff, far and wide. I actually remember the man who did that before Jeff took it over, a man we always used to call "Sheep" [William] MacDonald.   [NM]

There were a lot of different MacDonalds. So because he had a little bit of land and he kept some sheep he was always known as "Sheep" MacDonald. He was here first, I think, after the Indians. And then Jeff worked for "Sheep" MacDonald for a while.   [NP]

He was an old Scotsman, short and stout. He had whiskers. He used to drive an old horse and buggy with the mail and a stray passenger that wanted to go across and get to the CPR. And he used to land away out at the north end of Fairfield Island, away out on the MacDonald Road. That was before the Minto Landing, you see. There was no steamboat; it was all paddling. That's the way my father used to take his groceries across. And then MacDonald, he was drowned out there during high-water. He got caught in the current and away he went. Then Jeff Harrison took it over.   [JH]

From left to right: Captain R. Menton, engineer, and Jeff Harrison (PABC 60624).

It was very, very dangerous in wintertime when the ice was coming down the river, you know. People that never saw a canoe, nor anything else would get off the train and get into this canoe, and naturally they were very, very scared. Jeff used to get a big kick out of that. [NM]

When MacDonald was drowned, Bob Menton went in with Jeff, and they had this little *Minto* boat at what was called the Minto Landing. One time I was coming home in the middle of the winter from spending a holiday with relatives on the coast, and I said, "How in the world will we ever get on to the *Minto*?" because the ice had been forming and forming and was solid next to the shore, you see.

Jeff said, "Oh, you'll get on all right. We'll lay planks over the ice out to the boat."

So I walked over those planks, and that seemed to be all right. But when we arrived at the Minto Landing, for some reason Jeff couldn't bring that boat right up close to the ice. As you stepped off the boat there would be water and then this sheet of ice. I was really petrified with fear.

So Jeff said, "Don't you worry one bit. I'll get you there all right."

So they shoved some planks on the ice, and then a long heavy plank to the deck of the *Minto*. I stood there on this little deck, and I was looking at this cold ice and cold water when my cousin, Jeff, who was a big strong fellow, picked me up and carried me in his arms and walked across the plank over to the plank on top of the ice, and stood me down.

"Now," he says, "you did all that worrying for nothing." [NP]

They used to handle a lot of fruit, crated fruit. They'd connect with the CPR and supply the market back on the Prairies. That was before they got the ferry up at Agassiz. The *Minto* was just a weeny little boat, you see; they wouldn't take hay or grain or anything like that, just small stuff. But when they got the big ferry up at Rosedale and Agassiz, they could go right on to the ferry. [JH]

FLOODWATERS

Swinging the river

When I was a boy, living on the old homestead, which lies out here just a mile south of the Fiver Corners, there never was a spring during high water season in which that front field, (which lies between the farm home building and the highway), was not a lake. It was in that field at high water time that I learnt to swim at a very early age. I also learnt how to row a boat properly and paddle an Indian *canim* in the Indian fashion. We used to drive stakes on either side of the road, because if you drove off one side too much, and the old democrat just about floating, why the chances were you would *killapie*, as the Indians would say*.

Extreme highwaters were known as floods, and the first flood that my parents experienced was the flood of 1876. That was the highest water experienced by the white population up to that time. A few years after came the flood of 1882. That was the flood which I used to hear my parents talk about so much. When the water would start to back up in the Chilliwack River, which bounded our homestead on the south, my mother would say, "Oh, dear! I hope we won't have another '82." [JM]

Having to contend with a greater or lesser amount of annual high water was a relatively straightforward problem. The solution was to build dykes. But the rampages of the Chilliwack River, either in the spring or the fall, were rather more complex, since the whole flood plain was, in a sense, its creation.

In the early days there used to be a heavy snowfall every winter. The mountains were all timbered; they weren't half-logged off like they are today. And there was a big runoff every spring. People today don't realize what that river used to be like. There've been two bridges gone out at the Vedder Crossing. And you take right above the bridge today—that big gravel bar that lays in there used to be a darn good farm— Joe Teskey's. There was a 40 acre hay field there, a great big barn. The whole works went down the river one freshet, took her right out. And there used to be a small hotel there at the riverside, where that little riverside store is now; and there was a big cement tennis court. They all went down the river. That was about 1910 or 1916. [RW]

As mentioned earlier, when the valley was first settled the main section of the river on emerging from the hills, swung sharply to the north and was navigable by canoe almost all the way to what is now called Vedder Crossing. A very short distance to the west were the openings to the Luckakuck and Atchelitz branches, and for part of the last century all three streams carried some of the water and "started off just like your three fingers," as one of the local people put it.

In the fall of 1875 it rained nearly every day from the middle of October until the middle of November, then snowed for two days to a depth from two to three feet. A Chinook wind came up and the snow soon disappeared, even from the mountains. About November 22 the Chilliwack was the highest ever known, even up until this day. I had just started to live on the Sicker farm, opposite to Mr. Wells. That night the water in the Coqualeetza, as it was then called by the Indians . . . rose very fast. Mrs. Webb and I were spending the evening at Mr. Wells'. We stayed very late watching the stream rising and the banks washing away.

---

* Chinook jargon: *canim* = canoe; *killapie* = overturn.

A bridge across the stream, about forty feet long, we felt sure would be gone before morning, so I proposed to Mr. Wells that we take the covering off . . . as it was made of extra good split cedar. We took it all off, Mrs. Wells holding the lantern for Mr. Wells and Mrs. Webb for me. Our work was all lost, for in the morning everything belonging to the bridge was gone, covering and all, the stream being over 100 feet wide. This same night it broke through into the Vedder Creek.   [HW-1]

"A glimpse of the Vedder River" (PABC 77919).

Up to that time Vedder Creek had been no more than a small brook originating at the foot of Vedder Mountain, and running through the Vedder family's farms into Sumas Lake. Two years before, it had been muddied by a temporary trickle from the larger stream. In 1875 the flow seems to have been a bit more obvious. But the main worry was still the swollen Luckakuck and the damage it was doing to the farms along its banks. Together with Atchelitz Creek it was carrying most of the water, while the old river bed to the east was drying up.

As a consequence of the Fraser's big flood of the following year, the provincial government brought in a well-known civil engineer, Edgar Dewdney, to look into the question of flood control. He recommended two series of dykes: one to deal with the eastern section of the valley, which presented a particularly difficult problem, because of sloughs and seepage from the mountains, the other for the more settled western area, which was easier to handle. As for the Chilliwack River, he recommended it be directed into one main channel, namely the Luckakuck, which was carrying half the water, anyway, at that time; even though he knew quite well what the Sardis people thought about that. In fact, he mentioned that A. C. Wells "did not see why he should be compelled to take the balance, as it would be the means of ruining his farm."

In spite of these recommendations, nothing was done. Not only were they too costly for those days, but they were stirring up latent rivalries, Sardis and Chilliwack versus Sumas, which most people preferred to keep under the rug. The problem remained, however, because every time the Chilliwack River went on the rampage, and this was as likely to happen during the fall rains as during the spring thaws, debris could block up one or more of its exit channels, forcing it to find another outlet, playing havoc with the farms along its path. Those who lived near the Luckakuck or Vedder Creek, prayed their fields would not become a boggy mess for the spring or winter sowing, or simply be carried away altogether. What was good for Sardis was a disaster for Sumas, and vice versa*.

---

* "Whichever way the river went," said Oliver Wells, "within three miles it would fall 60 feet. And that gave it tremendous cutting power."

Not long after the breakthrough of 1875 a logjam was formed at the entrance to the Luckakuck, with the result that the Chilliwack was diverted more than ever into Vedder Creek. And as the land around Sardis was beginning to dry up, and more people were settling there, it was thought that nature could do with a little assistance.

> In 1882 some of the people of Sardis hired a man to drop a tree across the mouth [entrance] of the Luckakuck. It practically reached across the mouth of all three of the streams; they were only a short distance apart. It was a huge tree, some two or three hundred feet long. That's what I'm told. It formed a jam that blocked all three of the streams. And, of course, when there's a big freshet on, soon many stumps and logs come down, and they lodge in this thing. Then it will soon fill with gravel, you see.
> Now this remained a secret for many years—who dropped this big fir tree across the river. It was many years later, when my father was sitting in the Royal Hotel, when a Swedish man came up to him, and he said, "You're Samson Toop, are you?"
> And he said "Yes." And the man made himself known.
> "Well," he says, "you remember that there was a big fir tree dropped across the head of the three rivers, that diverted the water down onto Sumas?"
> And Dad says, "Yes. I remember quite well. But we never learned," he says, "who dropped that tree. It was a huge fir tree, over six feet through at the butt."
> "Well," he says, "I'm the man who dropped that tree. And I was paid well for it by certain parties in Sardis."
> That was during the high water of 1882, when the first water broke through and came down into the [Sumas] lake. You can readily understand that when the water starts over a piece of property it wouldn't form a channel at once. It would run in different directions on the lower land, you see.   [FT]
> Unfortunately it swept down towards Sumas, and land which had been well-drained land became boggy and swampy, and also the river did tremendous damage in cutting away land acreage. So it became a very sore point among the settlers; there was quite a conflict as to whether nature was swinging the river by its own causes, or whether the settlers were swinging the river one way or another by the use of powder or logjams.
> I believe the people of Sardis looked at it in the manner in which the river was naturally going, at least, I was brought up to believe that the river, through a jam, would take its natural course; and any effort from the Sardis point of view was that they were simply trying to prevent the river from being molested.   [OW]

Then it seems that one night, very secretly, the log pile was dynamited, causing damage to the Sardis farms. And when, in February 1889, the Sardis people attempted to restore the dam, they were met by a group from Sumas who were apparently carrying guns. So the Sardis people obtained a temporary injunction restraining their adversaries from interfering further with the natural course of the river, and brought an action against them, claiming $10,000 damages, and asking that the injunction be made permanent.

But it depended on what was meant by "natural". The defendants not only claimed that it was natural for Chilliwack waters to flow down the Luckakuck—as they had between 1875 and 1883—but that the dam on the Luckakuck had not been natural, in other words, it had been more or less manufactured.

Furthermore, they maintained that they had not dynamited it, but that the river itself had washed it away.

Mr. Justice McCreight must have had a difficult time sorting out what actually happened from the welter of accusation and innuendo. But sometime the following year he decided for the defendants, namely that the injunction should be set aside and that the Sardis people should pay all the costs of their action. Yet for some reason the Sumas people never got around to removing the logjam. Possibly it had already been partially washed away, so a certain amount of water continued to flow down the Luckakuck. Perhaps everyone felt the matter should rest until the next crisis. They didn't have long to wait.

The pews were dancing on the water

The spring of 1894 was cold, wet and backward, preventing the proper run-off from the snow on the mountains. Then towards the end of May the weather turned hot and sultry,

hot nights, as well as hot days, which is unusual for Chilliwack. I remember the Ontario boys, who used to come to the valley to work on farms, used to say, "My, what a glorious climate. The nights are cool and a fellow can rest and sleep after a hard day's work!"   [JM]

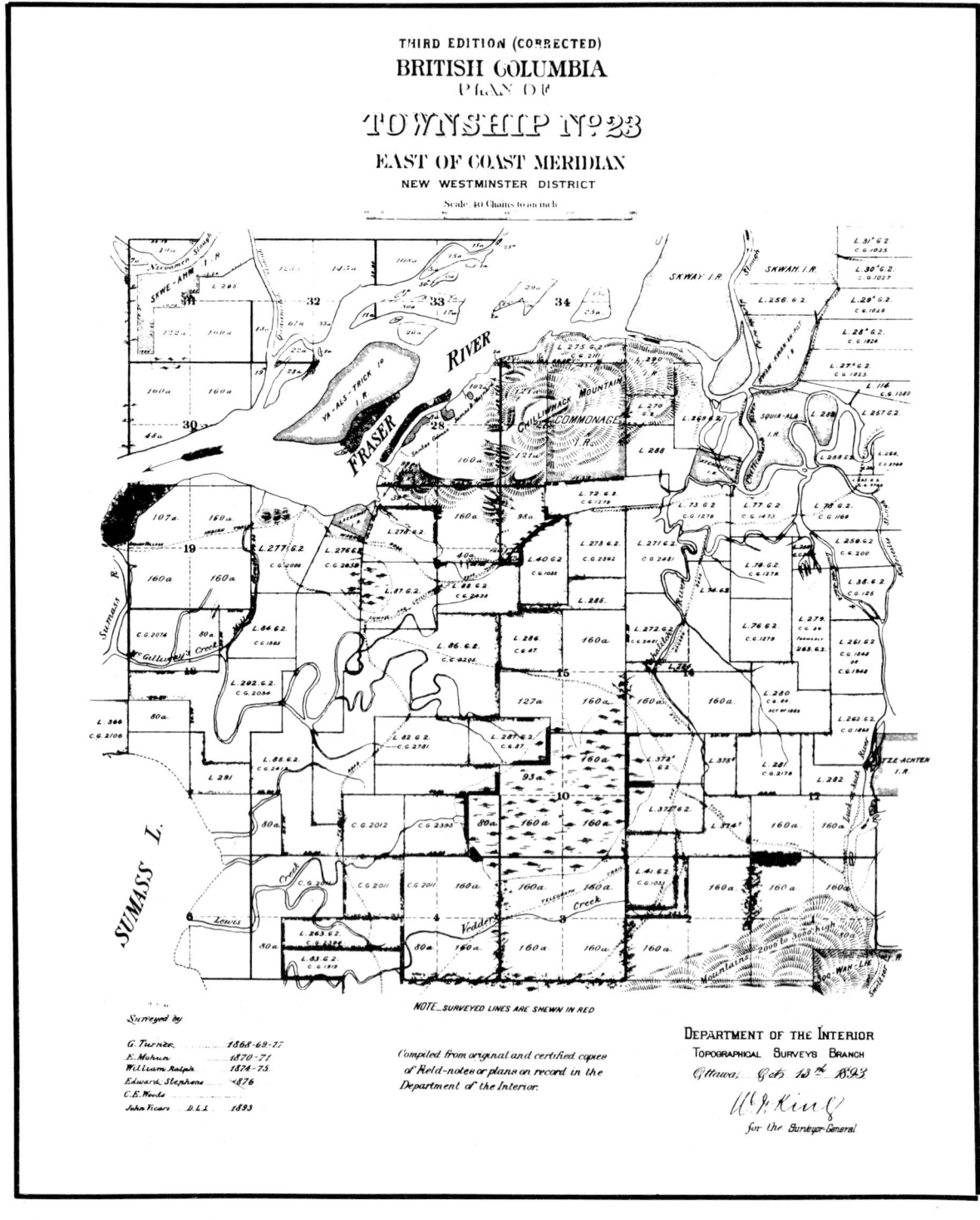

We get some idea of the disaster that was creeping up on them from a diary kept by a farmer's wife, who lived on the prairie at the far end of Sumas Lake. She had three small children to take care of, and another was born shortly after the water went down. Both she and her husband, Will Fadden, were used to coping with the annual highwater, and her laconic entries suggest there was no panic. May 23rd, a Wednesday, is a "very hot, fine day," and the expected high water is "coming up right along." Nevertheless, they do some gardening, and the next day go to a house-raising bee, instead of the usual 24th May picnic. On the 25th, it's "warmer than ever. Water rising fast." On the 26th they are planting corn.

The next morning they note that the "water reached last year's mark some-time during the night" and "was running in our ditch by the house." On Monday the 28th, Will Fadden went to the mill to get some lumber, to build a boat, while "Nell got wagon to take calves to Abbotsford. Water rising fast, about 1-3/4 inches an hour. Coming in garden a little." The next day they start building the boat, and the water is "spreading over garden, over orchard, quite high. Fine day." The following day, Wednesday the 30th their boat was finished enough to use. The water is now "all over orchard, garden, potatoes and everything. Hard times for stock to get enough dry land to sleep on."

While the water was creeping silently over these marginal farms, in the Chilliwack and lower Sumas areas the swollen rivers and streams were tearing at their banks. It was a far more critical situation.

> The old farmers would come to town and make a beeline for the telegraph office to enquire of my father as to how the water was acting up in the Cariboo. My father would read them dispatches, which he had received during the day from Soda Creek, Quesnel, the Nechako and Thompson Rivers. And the farmers would walk out shaking their heads, because they knew they were in for a flood.
>
> The water continued to rise, and it became necessary to move the stock off Sumas Prairie. The stock had bunched up on the high ridges, and it was necessary to swim them for home. Then it became necessary to move the stock to the farm occupied by James Mercer, father of Alex Mercer. And I have heard Alex say that when our herd was added to their herd he thought, with the exception of taking time out to eat, he was milking cows all day long. [JM]

We learn from the *Chilliwack Progress* of May 30th "The Luck-a-kuk and Chilliwack have both overflowed their banks and inundated tracts of lands, and the unusual body of water flowing down the Fraser has had the effect of backing the water into various streams tributary to it and damaging much property. Bridges have been wholly or partially swept away, and a few cattle have been drowned. Farmers in the low lying districts have in many cases moved their stock to higher lands, large tracts in places being under water. . . . There is good reason, however, for believing that the worst is over, and that the waters will soon recede. . . ."

They could do with a bit of optimism. The next day over at Upper Sumas the Faddens drove their stock across the line into the States. The night of Friday, June 1st, there was a sudden wind storm, with rain, thunder and lightning, and the next morning fences and other things were afloat, and "water all over downstairs." Their daughter, Joy, remembered how they

> lived downstairs for a little while, when it was about six inches to a foot, and then had to go upstairs. It was quite a time getting food to eat, and getting meals and things like that. Wynn, being the baby, my mother would put him upstairs to sleep. When he'd get over his sleep and come down, we'd find him sitting in the water. There were wooden wash-tubs on the back porch, and my brother, Angus, and I used to sail in them, and often capsized and got wet, too. So my mother had a double dose of drying out clothes. [JS]

As the telegraph line was down, there was no way of getting a message through to New Westminster for a stern-wheeler to come to the rescue. So Sam Cawley, Chilliwack's popular reeve, decided to go himself. Someone writing anonomously to the *Chilliwack Progress* paper many years later recalled how "on June 2, Saturday, he got together a crew of men who volunteered to go by boat down the raging river. . . . They started on this dangerous mission at 4:30 in the afternoon of June 2; five men, none of whom in the widest stretch of the imagination, could have been called a riverman; their craft was a little fishing boat with two sets of oars. Sixty four years ago the only other way to New Westminster was by horse-drawn vehicle or on horseback. And I am quite sure they got there a lot faster the way they chose to go, because they arrived in New Westminster at 9:35 that same night! All five of these men had extremely painful blistered hands, mute evidence of a contest which might very well have turned out in favour of the river, because that evening, during their frightening passage, a very violent storm came up, and they were continuously having to steer clear of driftwood and fallen trees being carried along on the flood-swollen river.

"At 2:00 a.m. on the morning of June 3, Sunday, they were able to procure the services of the steamer *Gladys,* and in her they started at daylight to make the return trip. They called at different places along the way, leaving tents, provisions, and lumber for building housing for stock. . . . They moored at the Chilliwack landing at 4:15 p.m. . . ." [*Progress*; 25 June 1958].

Actually, it was another little steamboat, the *Courser,* which stopped along the way. The *Gladys* had the Hon. Colonel Baker, the Provincial Secretary, on board, and when it got back three days later the purser gave an account of their trip to The *Daily Columbian*.

"We left port," he said, "at 3 o'clock on Sunday morning, proceeded direct to Hope Slough, where, finding no assistance required, the *Gladys* steamed back to Chilliwack. Here we loaded 40 head of cattle from Isaac Kipp's ranch, and Monday morning steamed right across country, passing over Sweatman's farm, to A. C. Wells' farm, which is above water. Returning, we took a load of fodder to Shannon Mountain on Hope Slough. At 5 o'clock, Tuesday morning, we ran up to the head of Camp Slough to Thorburn's ranch and removed a lot of horses, cattle, furniture and other goods to Shannon Mountain. Fifty ladies accompanied us and had an enjoyable picnic. Wednesday morning the *Gladys* steamed up to Mr. De Wolf's ranch on Camp Slough, but, as the water had fallen four inches, Mr. De Wolf decided not to remove his cattle. At noon yesterday, the work of relief being over, we headed for New Westminster. . . ." [*Columbian*, 7 June 1894].

> On the 9th of June the flood reached its height, and by that time the water was two feet seven and a half inches high over the floor in our big old farm house. The town was nearly all under water—an odd patch of road at the Five Corners. A favourite spot to land canoes and boats was in front of the Empress Hotel, as it now stands. The water held that high mark for several days.   [JM]
>
> Isaac Kipp's farm was a regular sea. The boats came, right up and took cattle out of the barns. Water all over the strawberries, but everybody seemed to be happy; they didn't seem to take it bad. Nobody had any money; there was no money to lose. You always had lots to eat.   [JH]

That's how it looked to a boy of 13. In fact, the ladies' "enjoyable picnic" suggested that it was not all gloom and doom, and people were adjusting. Youngsters like Jack Henderson and Jack McCutcheon, who was 14, were getting quite a kick out of having their little town turned into an instant Venice. The weather was warm, so was the water. An occasional ducking was a harmless diversion.

> There happened to be living in Chilliwack at that time a couple of young fellows, Walt Bradshaw and Jack Knight. They built themselves a flat-bottomed boat; and they paddled around town and were most accommodating in taking people from one dry part to another. But the strange part of it was that, for no accountable reason, the boat would upset and the passengers get a good ducking. I remember one day they very

View of the Chilliwack flood of 1894; taken from the Presbyterian Church (PABC 43260).

graciously offered to transport a very proper Englishman, Mr. Whitley, a bank clerk, over a stretch of water on Main Street. At that time there was a deep swale extending along the side of the road, and, would you believe it, that boat turned upside down in the deepest place. Mr. Whitley managed to reach the picket fence, which he frantically grasped hold of, but the pickets gave way as fast as he grasped them, and he stripped the fence for about three rods before he struck bottom. You were never safe when you rode with those fellows.

We did a lot of boating. There was a big fish boat moored out in front of the Empress Hotel, owned by an Indian at the Landing. I don't know whether the council rented it from him, or not. Anyway, it seemed to be at the disposal of anyone who wished to use it. It had accommodation for 30 people and was equipped with six oars, three on either side, so that six could row, and it was also equipped with a rudder. I remember one excursion in particular, because I was rudder man and steered the boat. We started out for Sumas to see how things looked there. We rowed down to Dave Chadsey's, and looking south and west Sumas Prairie looked like the Pacific Ocean. There was a stiff breeze blowing, and the waves were rolling in six feet high. I steered the boat over to the old McGillivray house, south of Dave's, out on the prairie, and we had a talk with a couple of McGillivray boys who were living upstairs. They had their heads out of the upstairs window, and the waves were spraying them. After spending a few minutes there, we turned the boat, and I steered for the Methodist church and, by the way, that church is still standing there. We rowed right into the church, and there were the pews and seats dancing on the water. We backed out, and I steered for home again.

Every other day or so I would paddle my canoe over to our farm, where my brother, Will, and the hired man were living upstairs. On this trip I was paddling south on Young Street. I noticed an object bobbing up and down a couple of hundred yards ahead of me and thought it was a dog at first. But when we met, it was a man. He swam up to the canoe, held on to the side, and we had a talk. The man was Mark Huff, who farmed on Brooks Ave. He said he had no boat. It was a nice warm day, he was a good swimmer, so he thought he would swim to town, for a change.

On another occasion I was paddling back from the farm by way of the Yale Road when I caught up to two men in a boat. One man was rowing, and the man sitting in the stern was Reeve Sam Cawley, and he was holding the head of a yearling colt in his lap. They were towing it to dry land to try and save the half-drowned animal. [JM]

"Mr. S. Cawley, the Reeve of the municipality, has been incessantly employed, either in steamboat, canoe or rowboat, toiling and laboring to rescue and assist wherever help was needed, largely to the neglect of his private business. This is the sort of men we want as our representatives—men who in time of emergency will devote their time and talents to the public weal. . . ." [*Progress*; 25 June 1958].

As for the Fadden family, when the water got near the top of the baseboards in the downstairs rooms, they pulled out and went to stay with some friends over at Huntingdon.

> My mother took the children, and she started to row across the prairie with us. Then this man, Blair, met her part way and helped her the rest of the way. He had a better boat. Father didn't go with her that morning. He was looking after too many things at home, I think. I never realized until after I had grown up how trying it must have been, with three small children and expecting a fourth one. [JS]

The water reached its height around June 7th, depending on where you lived, and stood more or less at a level for several days before it subsided.

> After a few days the land began to appear. And what a sight! The fields covered with dead vegetation and spoiled crops, rail fences floated away down the Chilliwack River back of our place, some of the floors of the house buckled up and covered with scum. Will and the hired man and I started to make rafts of the cedar rails and tow them back up to our place. Then we got into the boat and rowed to Bellrose on Vedder Mountain to start repairing the telegraph line, which ran along the edge of Sumas Lake in those days. [JM]

The Faddens moved back home on the 14th, and two days later they recorded that the water was falling fast and their garden was all clear. So they planted cucumbers and lettuce, set out the cabbage and extracted three quarts of honey. In another day or so the mosquitoes had mustered their forces and the windows had to be covered with cheese cloth. Will Fadden found his team across the line in Lynden, where another farmer had harnessed them to his plough.

The story in Lower Sumas, where the Chadseys lived, was rather different: "the whole district having the appearance of desolation that is sad to behold. . . . Mr. McGillivray's house is almost completely destroyed, the front being demolished. . . . Part of Mr. Chester Chadsey's house is gone, his outbuildings badly damaged. . . . Mr. G. Chadsey's house is full of water, the doors and windows broken. . . ." and so on. "Never before in the memory of man," said the editor of *The Progress*, rising to the occasion as usual, "has such a calamity occurred as the one which is now spread before our eyes in whichever direction we turn: and many a settler who congratulated himself upon a crop this season which would put him beyond the reach of want, finds his labor of the past in vain and the prospect black before him. . . ." [*Progress*; 13 June 1894].

> We sowed late barley, built a square silo in the barn and filled it with this barley. We bought and hauled some fifty loads of loose hay from Sheldon Knight of Sardis. We got no assistance from the government. How different to the treatment handed out to the flood victims of 1948. [JM]

> My father was among those who lost their farms following the 1894 flood. He had invested in a general store, thinking that it would serve the upper valley, rather than people having to come away down to the Landing to get supplies. And in 1894 we had no crop. There was no government help, as there is after a disaster now. So we moved to the Sardis area for a while. [NP]

For those who survived, however, the river waters proved to be a great fertilizer. "We had wonderful crops after that," said Jack Henderson, the storekeeper's son. "Killed all the vermin and everything."

And they had a trial

The flood of 1894 brought the Vedder affair to a head. It would seem that by then the creek had become the Chilliwack River's main outlet, with the result that the latter on leaving the hills was now known officially as the Vedder, and emptied most of itself into Sumas Lake. All of which was helped, no doubt, by one of those recurring logjams at the entrance to the Luckakuck, put there by mother nature, or otherwise.

In 1894, which was the biggest flood that was ever known here in the valley, a bunch of men decided to go and blow that jam and let the water back in its natural course. Well, while they were working there, preparing to put in a shot of dynamite, some of the people of Sardis saw them and notified the police. And he came out and had them arrested. They were taken into custody and locked up. And they had a trial. They sent for the judge, Judge Howay, and he heard the case, and he dismissed it. And he says, "Now, this stream will be purely and simply a government stream, and no corporation or individuals must tamper with this stream." And that's the way things lie to this day.

Now that river, the Vedder River, ruined several good farms. But it did a lot of good, too. For before the river came into the lake it was a very deep lake. There was over 40 feet of water in some parts of that lake.   [FT]

What Frank Toop is saying is that the silt from the Chilliwack-Vedder River helped to fill in Sumas Lake and contributed to the great fertility of the lake bed when it was drained. But the authorities very nearly had an old-fashioned feud on their hands, and even today, how the local people look at it could depend on which side their forebears were on. As one old-timer remarked, "There had been charges made that the river was changed. But, personally, I have some very good friends on both sides of the fence, and I wouldn't want to comment."   [FZ].

This farmland was formerly Sumas Lake (PABC 66503d).

A wildcat scheme

The 1894 flood was followed two years later by yet another large flood, fortunately it was not quite so destructive; but it was plain that dyking of the Fraser could not be postponed any longer. It had been a topic of conversation for years, and people like the Kipps had been building private dykes to protect their own land. In 1889 two dyking schemes were proposed for reclaiming the whole or part of Sumas Lake, and one of them actually got underway. It appears to have been the brainchild of two brothers, John and Frank Lumsden, who had come in from south of the border and bought the original Vedder property where Yarrow is today. Donald McGillivray was in on it. So was David Miller, who was living in his big new stone house by the Fraser. He had already lost a 60 acre hayfield to the raging current and been forced to move his farm buildings. He backed a bank note for $10,000.

>They got an inspiration, and they were going to dyke Sumas, and they were going to do it with slip-scrapers; and that was in 1892. Donald McGillivray had 800 acres, and he was all for it; and David Miller, he had quite a bit of land, and he was also very keen on it. And they mortgaged their property to finance this scheme.   [FT]
>
>There was a survey, and there was actually some plans drawn; and they started clearing some of the land. But when they ran out of funds the government wouldn't back them, so they didn't have the money to go any further.   [FZ]
>
>Well, it was a wildcat scheme, because they should have known that they couldn't build a dyke with slip-scrapers that would hold out high water, because they had seen the '82, which was a baby compared to '94. And when the '94 flood came—well, they abandoned the whole scheme.   [FT]
>
>And Mr. Miller lost everything he had. I can remember when the poor old man walked out of the house. He was on two canes, crippled up, and the tears streaming down his face. They moved over to where Kilgard is today, and he's buried there. He didn't last long after they moved away from here.   [FZ]

Finally the provincial government took over, and in 1899 the dyking of the Fraser began in earnest. For three years the Chilliwack and Sumas farmers, along with their horses, got much needed employment—and cash—with their ploughs and scrapers. After that the valley people felt a great deal more secure.

It was not till 1924 that the first plow was applied to the rich land that had been Sumas Lake. The man most responsible for this was a Chilliwack farmer, Edward Dodsley Barrow, who became Minister of Agriculture in 1919. By a curious coincidence, soon after his arrival in the valley, both he and his brother had worked on the right-of-way for that first abortive attempt.

TOWN AND COUNTRY

There was no cash

The floods of 1894 and 1896, which left their mark all over the lower mainland couldn't have come at a worse time for the Chilliwack Valley. The heady period of railway construction and the opening up of new markets, had quite suddenly come to an end the year before, due, as usual, to a financial crisis south of the border. In the little city of Vancouver, scarcely seven years old, there were soup kitchens and bankruptcies, and much unemployment and misery. The fishing and logging industries were particularly hard hit. The recession was somewhat easier on the farmers, as they could at least subsist; but some of them lost their farms, and even people like A. C. Wells found it difficult to make ends meet. He had just taken a big step forward in the construction of a large dairy barn, very modern for its time, which could hold 500 tons of loose hay and 100 head of cattle. Then the prices on all farm products dropped radically, and Wells, who had counted on selling large quantities of hay, couldn't even sell it for $5 a ton. "I hear that even he is going behind," commented a young chap, writing to his father in Ontario. He went on to note, "Ashwell and old Henderson are aging very fast, as they have so much money out on property that would not realize mortgage if sold, owing to drop in prices of land" [Wells; 5].

> Billy Atkinson, an old Ontario boy, who came to Chilliwack in those days, became a crack auctioneer and later [August 1928] became Minister of Agriculture for B.C. used to like to tell the story about the one dollar bill, which used to float around among us after the '94 flood. He said it changed hands so much that finally it became worn out. And then we did not have any money at all!   [JM]
>
> It was all barter. You'd take your butter into town, or your chickens or anything like that. There were two stores in Chilliwack, the G. R. Ashwell store and the Henderson store. They were general purpose stores. You'd take it in, and probably you'd have a credit the next time you went in; but there was no cash.   [CB]
>
> I remember mother often regretted the fact that she couldn't get cash for butter and eggs. They said, "No. We give you credit for those things." I can see my mother's face, the look of frustration, when he would say, "I'm sorry Mrs. Ryder, but we won't give you any cash. We'll give you credit. You can have flour and sugar and tea, and that sort of thing." Well, they sold shoes, too. They sold everything at Henderson's store. Which was very fine in a way, because you had to have these other things. But for the church giving, and for many little things, you want cash. And an Indian would come around with a beautiful salmon—just out of the cold water for 25¢. Well, if you didn't have the 25¢ you couldn't buy a salmon; and a salmon was quite a help when there was a big family.   [NP]

Farm wages were practically nil, but board and lodging was available for those who were willing to work at clearing, fencing and draining the land. This may have been the time when the Chinese would clear it simply for the use of it for two or three years. In fact, there was still a lot of clearing to be done, even on farms that were well established, but particularly so in the eastern sections where homesteads were still hemmed in by the forest, and accessible only by trails, winding through the trees.

> If you wanted to get out from here you had to go through the bush over to the Yale Road. There was a trail, and it came out on the Coverdale place, they called it. Once a year they used to shut the gate there for one day, so it couldn't be counted as a highway. Eventually the section roads got opened up, but they had to drain them, and still they were wet. I can remember going down the roads later on when they were all corduroyed—it was all horse and wagon at that time—and in winter there'd be big holes you'd have to go around; and sometimes you'd get stuck.   [CB]

Once the Fraser had been dyked the government proceeded to drain a large section of the East Chilliwack area. This was done by a floating dredge widening and deepening Semmihault Creek almost up to the foot of the mountains. After that ditches were dug, and there was a gradual drying up of that part of the valley.

$300 for a team of oxen

It takes quite a number of years for a newly cleared countryside to reach maturity, for the scars to heal and the second, and largely deciduous growth to acquire the uninhibited shapeliness we see today. From early photos it is plain the valley was still in transition; many fields were still bordered by a scattering of scraggy conifers, if not by thick conifer groves, relics of the original forest. Gradually the grid system was leaving its mark; wandering trails were being replaced by new roads and drainage ditches along the boundary lines. However, to someone in the 1890s coming from southern Ontario, where settlement had been going on for up to a hundred years, this was still a raw western landscape. In fact, the editor of the *Chilliwack Progress* took it upon himself to chastise the Chilliwack farmers for their untidiness. "We regret to see," he said, "the front portion of so many good farms have such a dissipated appearance: fences badly out of repair, and what would make tillable land allowed to grow with underbrush" [*Progress*; 10 Sept. 1891]. He didn't like snake fences, particularly when they were old and blackened. He didn't like the way some farmers would haul stumps and other rubbish onto the road and just leave it there. It seems that some farmers "would not plant shade trees because the leaves rotting in the fall could be unhealthy." He urged everyone to remove the rubbish from around their houses and surround them with gardens, walks and "neat picket fences." And these remarks were made before the recession, before the big flood of 1894.

In those days recessions came and went rather more quickly and easily than they do today, and by the end of the century the whole province was once more experiencing the economic expansion that had begun with the coming of the CPR. Some of it, naturally, rubbed off on the farmers of Chilliwack. A. C. Wells, writing to his son-in-law in England in 1897, remarks that the Kootenay mines had much improved their prospects. He hopes to get $10 a ton, FOB for his hay, whereas two years before he would have been lucky to receive $5 [*Wells*; 5]. In 1898 there was the excitement and stimulus of the gold rush into the Klondyke. The following year the Fraser River dyking began, which was another source of cash for the many farmers who worked on it. Not only was there great activity in the mines, railways being built, and so on, but the logging industry was thriving, and lumber mills were springing up all through the lower mainland.

> That provided a market for hay, and I imagine for dairy products. Farmers would get $300 for a team of oxen. They kept Durham cattle and the steers would provide big strong teams.   [OW]
>
> About 1904 or '5 a famous man came in here—a little old lame man by the name of Frank Colley. He used to travel the country with his horse and his wagon, and peddle through the valley. He would do quite a lot of buying in the way of pigs. You'd take them down to the Landing and have them shipped down to New Westminster live weight. And he was actually, in this part of the country, the only person who ever gave anybody any cash.

Other than pigs, there was quite a good sale for horses at that time. All transfers at the coast were done by horses. Father was a horseman more than a cowman. We raised a lot of draft horses, and it all brought in quite a lot of money.   [CB]

Years ago several of us farmers used to stall-feed steers all winter. Al Evans used to ride up over the Hope-Princeton Trail every fall and drive over the Allison Pass a bunch of range cattle and stall-feed them, too. Then in the spring we would sell them to some Vancouver butcher. And we would join together and have a big cattle drive to the steamboat late in March. There was always quite a time in loading them at the lower bar. We used to use a steer every winter on our farm to run the treadmill, which supplied the power to run the turnip cutter. This steer naturally became quite well broken, and would lead anywhere; and he sure came in handy when it came to loading those steers on the steamboat. We'd lead him down the gangplank—gates on either side, of course—and that would entice the rest to follow.

This particular spring the steers had all been bought by old Jake Grauer, a butcher at the coast; and we were loading them at the lower bar, because the boat could not get up to her regular landing, because of low water. Al Evans' steers were always hard to handle, being range cattle, and they were hard to hold on the bar, as there were no corrals. And two of them broke loose and ran into the bush. There was not time to hunt them out of the bush, because the boat was due to leave at seven a.m. and it was long past that time already.

Old Jake was on the boat, and when he saw what had happened, he hollered out to Al, "Say, Allie, what are we going to do about it? You'd better buy those steers back."

Al, the artful fellow, said, "No, I don't want them. I have lots more home."

Chilliwack Livery Feed and Sale Stables. Man on far left is Jack Stevenson; man in centre is Al Chadsey (PABC 77930).

Then Jake shouted, "Well, can't you give me something for them, Allie?"

Al thought for a moment and then he shouted, "Yes, Jake. I'll trade you this horse I'm riding for them."

Jake said, "All right."

Al pulled the saddle off the horse, and the deckhands, after a lot of trouble, got the horse on board. The boat tooted, cast off her moorings, and started for New Westminster. Al got his men to run the steers out of the bush and drive them home.

Al told me afterwards about this horse. He said of all the devils in horseflesh he thought this horse was the worst. He said he would let you ride him, that is, if you were a good rider and could stand some bucking, but anything else, no.

It was six months or more before he saw old Jake Grauer again. When he met him, he said, "Say, Jake, how did that horse we traded for the cattle work out?"

A pained expression came over Jake's face. He said, "By gosh, Allie! You sure puts it to me that time! We hitched him up in one of our butcher carts."

Now these carts were ideal for breaking in horses to drive. They were very strongly built and were high over the horse; and the butcher boys who drove these carts figured they could handle any horse in one.

"Well," Jake said, "that horse ran away so many times with the boys, smashing things up, breaking the harness and kicking so many carts to pieces, that they finally gave him up for a bad job and turned him out to pasture. "Yes," Jake said, "you sure puts it to me that time, Allie." [JM]

Father's favourite sport was trading horse. I can remember going to town with him out through the bush here. It was a full day, and I've seen him trade the horse three or four times before he got home. As long as he lived he always had a horse he could trade with.

I can see them yet. They'd meet each other on the road and start in to talk horses; and they'd start to trade. It was more or less a sport, and some people were good traders. But even these got beaten sometimes. They kept one good horse that they were sure of getting home with, and they had one trading horse. Usually the horse that they traded, there was something wrong with it. It balked, it would run away, or it would back up in the stall; or sometimes they were winded, sometimes they had bad legs or spasms. Those old boys at that time, when they went off on a trading spree, knew how to dress a horse up a little bit that didn't show just what was the trouble with it. If the one that you got had worse habits that the one you gave away, well, you knew you'd got beaten. Any time both sides think they win, that's a good deal. And they'd laugh at each other—it was all a sport. The part I always got the kick out of, when I was a little older, was that they never traded the good horse. [CB]

We had some great sport

The young people had a meeting once a week. Everybody used to go, and it was usually on Friday night. At that time they were so strict there was no dancing allowed; that was taboo entirely, and card playing was taboo. And that filled in a terrific social gap for the young people—debating and plays, all kinds of games, a lot of sing-songs. And it wasn't too cliquey at all; everybody joined in. There were usually one or two of the older folks who came along and helped out, chaperoned, or whatever you want to call it. They'd meet in the church, then they eventually built a hall. There were strawberry festivals and Sunday school picnics and maybe a church picnic; and everybody went. [CB]

Vedder Crossing was a favourite place for holding picnics. The old farmers would drive across the bridge, turn to the left and drive into a nice cottonwood grove which existed there in those days. They would unharness their horses, tie them in the shade, throw them an armful of hay, and then proceed to assist the womenfolk in preparing a picnic lunch. And what a luncheon! What prodigious appetites those old-timers had. After lunch the young fry would hit for Cultus Lake by way of the wagon road to the Cultus Lake Indian reservation, and then follow a trail through the woods to the lake. The old folks would remain at the Crossing, clear up after the lunch, and then settle themselves comfortably in the shade and proceed to enjoy a real old pioneer reunion. [JM]

There was a little road went up through the Indian settlement there, not much more than a trail. A wagon could just wind through the woods to get to the lake. There were no buildings at all when I first went there, because the timber companies wouldn't allow them a franchise to build there. It was all timber limits right up to the lake. [JK]

Jack McCutcheon in centre with pole; 1896 (McCutcheon photo).

Every year, as soon as the haying was finished, there was a day off. My grandfather took the team and wagon and democrats and most of the families; and there'd probably be 10 to 20 men who had worked during the haying. And everybody'd go to Cultus Lake for a day's holiday; get up at four o'clock in the morning and milk out about 85 cows and do the chores up, get away about half past seven and head for Cultus Lake, and get there before noon. And you'd have about four hours to spend. Then you'd have to get back and go to milking again. And that was an annual event.

You could just drive the team down to the lake, and tie them up to a tree there. And it didn't matter whether anybody had bathing suits or not. The men would all go up one way and the ladies would all go down the other way, and everybody'd go in swimming. Nobody used bathing suits—well, they were hardly necessary. You'd never see the men and the women in swimming together, anyway.   [RW]

We had two baseball teams, Chilliwack and Rosedale, and keen rivalry existed between them. They were continually stealing a march on each other. First one side would import a professional pitcher and catcher, and then the other side would do the same. The kids were baseball crazy, too.

In those early days there used to be a lot of English remittance men knocking about. We called them all "chappies*". They seemed to have lots of time on their hands, and how they loved to kick the [soccer] ball—all handy players, having learnt the fine points of the game back home. These young men were nearly always available so, together with a lot of local boys, it was possible to field two teams if necessary. Our boys belonged to the Coast League, namely, Vancouver Celtics and the New Westminster Shamrocks. Our boys would go down to the coast and play these teams, and they would journey up to Chilliwack from time to time to return the compliment.

From the time I was 16 years old I competed in track events. For a number of years I would take my spikes and tights and travel to different places to compete. We had some good athletes, notwithstanding we had no training. Arthur Kipp was the champion at the track meets. He and I used to compete against each other.   [JM]

---

* A. C. Wells boarded young Englishmen who wanted to learn farming. This was a common practice at the time, particularly in the Okanagan, where they were called "mud pups". In the Chilliwack Valley "chappies" were not popular when it came to employing them.

69

But never on Sundays—not among the protestants, anyway. The young men who worked on the farms naturally kept themselves in trim, and any kind of national holiday or community gathering was an excuse for competitive sports. They were even part of the fun and games that accompanied an election in those days.

> Our first dominion election after Confederation, for New Westminster District, the polling station for the upper end of the district was held at the Marks place. Voters came from as far down as Matsqui and up as far as Agassiz. It was a great day. Some came in canoes and some on horseback. It was open voting and free drinks. We had some great sports, particularly with foot-racing between the last year's champion in the upper country, William Shannon, [and] William and George Chadsey from the lower country. [HW-1]
>
> Fifty-five or sixty years ago that portion of Isaac Kipp's farm where the arena and agricultural race track are located—that area, when I was a boy—was what we called Kipp's Lake. It extended for over a quarter of a mile, and when it froze over in winter, why there's where we did our skating. We built bonfires from the Kipps' cedar rails and had lanterns placed along the ice at intervals. The young people would come from far and near to Kipp's Lake. Arthur Kipp had a pair of wooden skates—steel blades, of course. They were held on by a screw in the heel and straps on the toes. And, of course, he was the fastest skater in the bunch. We would pile a lot of boxes and chairs on the ice and then watch Kipp jump over them. I used to hold my breath sometimes to see him soar through the air.
>
> In those days the horse racing was done on the Yale Road, or, as we call it today, the highway. There were two roads: the gravel road and a dirt road alongside. Horses with no shoes took the dirt road, and the starting place was McCutcheon's road gate, and the winning post was Kipp Lane gate, now called Hodgins Avenue. Built along the road from Hodgins Avenue west for about 100 yards was a board fence, and that was our grandstand. We would all climb up on this fence and sit on the top board, strung along the fence like the swallows on the telegraph wire.
>
> We would not see the start of the race because of a bend in the road, but now and then you would hear some over-anxious fellow holler, "Here they come!" There was a lot of false alarms. Finally, they really were coming around the bend, and then the excitement began. And just before the horses crossed the winning line the board fence would give way, and the old farmers would go heels over head backwards into Ike Kipp's field. [JM]

The festive season

> Speaking of Kipp's Lane recalls to my mind that it was also called Lovers' Lane, because it was a favourite promenade for the sparks of those days. On a lovely summer Sunday afternoon you would see the couples strolling down Kipp's Lane, arm in arm, the gent holding the sun parasol over his ladylove to shield her from the sun tan. [JM]

What a delightful symbol that parasol is: it belongs to the lady, but the gent holds it, and so she is protected. The proprieties are upheld in the sight of all.

Jack McCutcheon goes on to say, "How different the custom today! They jump into a car, burn the road up for Cultus Lake, where they pull on an abbreviated swimming suit, and then lie on the beach and absorb all the sun rays and sun tan possible." But that sort of thing came about after the gradual social breakdown that began with the disillusionment of the First World War. What we're looking at here is a society on its way up to new levels of sophistication, confident that all will be well with a world in which people know the rules and stick with them. It was that same instinct for refinement that had led them to build a neat white house in the place of a log cabin, and in later years to relegate the kitchen to an addition at the back, so that one of the front rooms could be set up as a parlour. It put fringes on the democrats, corsets on the women and feathers in their ridiculous hats. So the social milieu of the first decade of the century was getting to be rather different from the one that emanated from the sober, hard-working, church-going people of 30 years before.

Every week or two during the winter season we would have a dance in some private home, not over 10 or 12 couples. There would be little dances like this all over the valley. Public dances were frowned upon in those days. We also had an assembly called the Maple Leaf Assembly, which held a dance every two weeks. It was a membership affair, and the member could bring a guest. The rules were strict. If anyone smelled of booze, that person was politely asked to leave. Miss Minnie Doesterheoft supplied the music, and Archie Kipp supplied the music for the house dances.

The crowning event of the festive season was the grand ball, given by the Masonic Lodge in Henderson Hall. That's where you would see some style. You were considered lucky to get an invite to the Masonic Ball. Each mason was allowed to invite two guests. You presented your invitation to the man at the door and if it was in order, he handed you a pretty little booklet containing the dance programme. You opened the booklet, and there was the number and name of each dance, usually 24. A delicate little pencil is attached to the book by a silk string, and you walk around the hall and fill out your programme before the dance commences. You walk up and ask a young lady if you might see her programme, then you ask if you might have the pleasure of dance number 10. It is the Jersey. If she says, "Yes," she writes your name opposite Number 10 on her programme, and you write her name in your programme opposite Number 10, Jersey. So before the dance begins, you know who you are going to dance each dance with, though, if you are wise, you will have a few dances open for late arrivals.

Dress suits were the order of the day—great white shirt fronts, stiff as a board, white kid gloves. And if you saw a "chappie" whose suit was too small or too big for him, the probabilities are he got the loan of it from Colonel Coote, who always had a half dozen suits for such occasions. The ladies wore nice decent ball dresses, medium low neck, and many of them carried fans.

The orchestra would strike up the 'Grand March,' and after the dancers had marched around the hall a couple of times the orchestra stopped, couples would form into sets of four, and the beautiful square dance known as the Lancers would begin. Special Lancers music was played by the orchestra, nobody calling off: four different changes, and different music written for each change or figure. A very lovely dance when danced properly.

Here's a list of some of the dances on the programme: Jersey, Bonton, Ripple, French Minuet, Spanish Waltz, Carmeleta, Two Step, One Step, etc. We had two dancing instructors: Professor Myers of Harrison Mills, and Danny Nicholson. So when your programme said that number 12 would be the Jersey, why, you danced the Jersey as distinguished from any other dance. My father used to tell us that when he was a boy in Tipperary, Ireland, the dancing master used to make regular calls at their homes to teach step dancing to the younger people.

Sleigh-riding parties used to be very popular when I was a boy—four horse teams hitched to bobsleighs with a deep long box, lots of nice clean straw and plenty of rugs and blankets. We used to do a lot of singing on those rides, and what a chime the sleigh bells made. One of these rides I will never forget. The teams used were my brother Will's and Ed Reece's, and our destination was Popkum, twelve miles from Chilliwack—and that awful Popkum Bluff to climb. We were going to visit the Will Knight family at Popkum, have a little party, dance, etc. The sleighing was not so good, as the weather was moderating fast. When things were in full swing, someone came in and said it was starting to rain. So we cut our visit short and started for home. What a trip! A warm chinook wind melting the snow fast, and the rain pouring down. The horses had to pull the sleighs over bare spots in the road, the men walking. When we reached home that night the horses were in a white lather, and my brother Will spent until daylight cooling the team off, rubbing them down and blanketing them to save them from becoming foundered. [JM]

Jolly Boys

Those were the days when every respectable town had a band to lend pomp and circumstance to parades and other public occasions, The Queen's Birthday, Dominion Day, fall fairs and so on. Chilliwack arrived at the required maturity sometime in the 1890s.

Bob Marshall was the first bandmaster here. I was going to his place once, and I was whistling away, you know,—I used to be tearing about, always whistling. And he said, "Come on in here, Jack." And I went in.
"We're starting a band." he said. "I want you to come into it."
"Oh, I can't." You know the way a fellow is.
"Come on up next Tuesday night."
So I went up. I got a horn right there. I think he started me on a valve trombone. And we had quite a nice little band, you know.   [JH]

Fifty years ago we had no less than four bands in Chilliwack. There was the Silver Cornet Band, the Chilliwack Brass Band, the Coqualeetza Band at Sardis, and also a cracking good Indian band at the Landing reservation. This Indian band was the result of the training received at the mission school for young Indian boys at Mission. When the young fellows came home, why, they started a band of their own.

You could hear a band concert any nice summer Sunday afternoon, if you went down to the Landing reservation. A football game would be in progress, and the band would play at intervals. Sometimes they would hold their celebrations on the bank of

Local band at fairgrounds, Chilliwack (PABC 43184).

Koquapilt Slough on the Koquapilt Reserve. Every Saturday afternoon Robert Marshall would walk out to Sardis and have band practice at the Coqualeetza School. But the most progressive and perhaps the best band was the Chilliwack Brass Band, which held together for many years. Robert Marshall was our bandmaster. [JM]

Didn't play any hard stuff. All old Southwell music, real easy mucic. 'Jolly Boys,' I can remember that; that was our favourite, written by George Southwell. I think we played that 'Over the Waves' waltz. But 'Jolly Boys,' that was our old standby. We could play that in the dark. After every strain it would be "dah-dah—dah-dah-dah." We sure thought we were right into the classics when we got into that. [JH]

We financed our band by giving a band concert every year. We were also hired to play at all church garden parties given during the summer. We would ride around in our bandwagon on New Year's Day and serenade the village, and pick up a few dollars that way. Ed Reece used to drive us around with his team. We played for the fall fairs and other celebrations. We always looked forward to the annual excursion to the Harrison Hot Springs on the 24th May, given under the management of the Sardis Sunday School, and open to anyone who bought a ticket. [JM]

The whole family, the whole jim-bang, would go—girls and boys and everything. There were no automobiles then. They'd all come with their teams and tie them up down at the Landing, get on board and away they'd go. They had a basket picnic, you see—stay up there all day.

We'd all get up to the front of the boat there and play; put a little culture in on the way up. They had a big hotel up there called the St. Alice Hotel, and the old fellows would get up there and play billiards. They had a saloon and quite a lot of them got soused. Coming back there'd be a lot of rows, and two or three fights, and one thing and another. Oh, it was a lovely trip. We made good money on that. [JH]

On election days the band would be out to add to the noise and the enthusiasm. Those were the days of "Dick" McBride, who led his Conservatives to victory four times between 1903 and 1912.

Pretty near every political meeting there'd be a round up. They'd scrap it out right there. We used to have a hall, Henderson Hall, above our store. And there was none of this one fellow have a meeting here and another fellow have a meeting there. The two of them would get up, and they'd fight her out at dagger ends. They had to read the riot act there once; everybody was fighting. I remember A. C. Wells was chairman. He was a Conservative, and he gave his candidate a few more minutes than he give the other speaker. He had to answer some questions, or do something. And, boy-oh-boy, they were into it. There was a fight all the way down the stairs. Everybody was fighting.

Up in that old Henderson Hall I bet there'd be 200 men up there; not one woman, not one kid. When the speaker was on, you could hear a pin drop, but the big row that night was letting the government speaker speak a little longer than the opposition. [JH]

My father, being a dyed-in-the-wool Liberal from Ontario, had a great deal to say for a quiet man. And then maybe one of his neighbours who was a Tory, he had a great deal to say. So there would be fireworks for a while. The election was the big night. A procession would be formed; they'd have torches and music, and the winning candidate would be carried on their shoulders right through the village, up and down. The band would be out and the people would be cheering. Oh, there'd be a wonderful time. Election time in Chilliwack was really more colourful than it is today. [NP]

A peaceful sort of people

Chilliwack had come quite a way in thirty years or so. It was becoming quite a lively little town. A school teacher, who was there for a short time in the early 1870s, recalled how much she disliked the place. "Their mode of living," she said, "was altogether different from Port Douglas and Fort Yale. For one thing they were so religious; mostly all were Wesleyan Methodist*." So the place wasn't to everyone's taste, particularly if they had been brought up in some rip-roaring mining community in the days of the gold rush. On the other hand, one has to remember that these evangelical farmers had seen for themselves the drunkenness, brawling and social degeneration associated with the licensed saloons of their day, so it's easy to sympathise with their determination to keep their beloved valley different from the rest of the province—at least in that respect. But they ran into a lot of opposition.

> There was no licensed places, not that I heard of, until the government liquor stores were put in here. But this here Women's Christian Temperance Union, when they got organized they only made matters worse. They used to drink then, just to make them angry. There was Will Cawley [at the Queen's Hotel]. He had sort of a bar there, and they tried their best to get him ousted out of there, this Women's Christian Temperance Union. They got a detective from Westminster to try to catch him. And I'm darned if he didn't get that detective landed in jail or sent out of town. Oh land! He got him caught red-handed some way or other†. The rest of the population got so angry at this temperance union that they called them the "Worst Curse Turned Up." [JK]

And that's very much what happened. The sale of liquor was a local option, and the licensing authority was vested in a combination of local JPs and the municipal council, the majority of whom in the Chilliwack Valley were staunch Methodists or Presbyterians, and they were able to prevent any public sale of liquor until well into the present century. Anyone who wanted to drink socially, as opposed to drinking at home, had to join a club, for which, by law, there was quite a stiff fee. This discriminated against the poorer people. Naturally, there was some bootlegging; and liquor could be brought up on the boats, or across the line from Sumas City, where the bars were wide open. Jack McCutcheon spoke of how, "when the highwater was over, and a new growth of wild grass had grown to a fair height, the big ranchers would club together and start putting up wild hay in stacks. But before they started to cut they would buy a keg of whiskey and put it in a shack in the centre of the laying area," for when they got thirsty.

But back to our story. This Will Cawley was a respectable owner of several businesses in town, including the Commercial Hotel, which was later called the Queen's Hotel. And being an Anglican, he did not share the evangelicals' views about liquor; so that, when in 1892 the provincial government liberalised the law governing the sale of liquor, he tried to drum up support for a liquor licence for his hotel. This alarmed the opposition, and none other than the local Methodist minister arranged that a man called Abbot, pretending to be a traveller from the state of Washington with a toothache, should go to the Queen's Hotel and ask Cawley if he would sell him some liquor. Cawley gave him some, but firmly declined to take any money for it, in spite of Abbot's persistent efforts to pay him. Nevertheless, Cawley was charged with selling liquor. But in the course of his trial he succeeded in exposing Abbot as an agent provocateur, and the case was dismissed. Abbot was then fined for violating the liquor laws.

Later, in a letter to the paper, Cawley implicated the minister, and even charged the Reeve, A. C. Wells, with complicity. The minister fully admitted his devious activities, without, it seems, any misgivings whatsoever.

---

* Mrs. Josephine York, a letter in the Chilliwack Historical Society archives.
† For a more detailed variant of this story, see "Bibles and Booze," *BC Historical News*, April 1978, pp. 2–8.

Opposite: Camp River, Mt. Cheam in background (PABC 10373).

Not only did people not play games on Sunday, but they weren't even allowed to work at anything that wasn't absolutely essential. That was the law.

> The only person I ever saw fined was a poor old Chinaman, for hoeing his potatoes on Sunday. But they never said a word to the white people. I saw lots of them doing things they shouldn't be doing on Sunday. But they were all right; they were white people.   [JK]

Today, we can only deplore the way many of the pioneers regarded the Chinese people who were living amongst them, and so obviously playing a part in the growing prosperity of the country, clearing and draining land, constructing railways, engaging in various kinds of business. They were exceptionally honest and dependable, yet they were objects of fun, and the butt of an endless series of mean tricks practised on them by the children. Their only faults seem to have been that they dressed differently from other people, kept to themselves, and didn't belong to a Christian church.

> In those days they wore what we used to call a pigtail, a long braided silk-like black thing, that would hang down way below their knees, halfway down to their legs. And they used to raise potatoes a lot before the blight got in here.   [JK]
>
> It was no uncommon sight to see half-a-dozen Chinamen, one behind the other, travelling the road, their pack poles heavily loaded. There was a bunch of China shacks situated on the Young Road, just across from where the old courthouse used to be. There was also a bunch of China shacks just where the Chilliwack telephone office stands. And the Chinamen would travel from one Chinatown to the other to visit, gamble and smoke opium.   [JM]

We have to remember that certain racial prejudices, certain religious and social bigotries, were common to the Victorian era. It follows that the valley people had their share of them. But in other ways they could be genuinely progressive. They were second-to-none when it came to improving their crops, their livestock or their farm machinery. They went out of their way to foster a strong, viable community where only recently there had been little but floodland and primeval forest. When a printer turned up from Ontario to give the valley its first newspaper, the name he chose for it, the *Chilliwack Progress,* was no mere catchword.

They took advantage of the new province's school system as soon as it was set up, and little elementary schools began to appear in the various settlements. At least three of their sons were sent east to study at the Ontario Agricultural College at Guelph. But not till 1903 was a high school opened. Before that any young people wanting to complete their secondary education were obliged to find board and lodging in one of the coastal cities, which made it a bit of a luxury.

> My mother and father couldn't afford to send the older ones to New Westminster or Vancouver for a higher education. However, I attended the first high school, which was situated down where the Central School now stands, and there were just two rooms. I understand that before that the high school pupils had attended classes in Dr. McCaffrey's house.   [NP]

Opposite: Chilliwack Public School, 1900. J. McCutcheon and Mrs. S. Mellard (under the window on the left) and J. C. Henderson were trustees; the principal was W. M. Wood (McCutcheon photo).

The first sidewalk

Photos taken during the 1890s, when Centreville was becoming Chilliwack, show us a typical little western village with plenty of space between the buildings, a great deal of grass and weeds, even some stumps. The farms seem to be reaching right to the back fences; and as late as 1914 the city council was arranging for the grass on the boulevards to be cut for hay, and calling on householders to keep their horses and cows inside their own fences. Plainly, both the physical and psychological borderline between town and country was still somewhat vague.

We, whose ears are inured to the roar of traffic, would have found it a very quiet place. It would have been easy to distinguish one sound from another: the clop-clop of horses and their snorting: the commands of their drivers and the crack of whips: the rumble or squeak of wheels (buggies, democrats, wagons and carts) in the mud or the dust. It would be quiet enough to hear someone whistling at work, or people calling to each other across the street, quiet enough to hear their footsteps on the wooden sidewalks—where there were any.

The first sidewalk they ever had was from the Five Corners down to Hazel Street. It was just one plank put on end of another one, a single plank. Then they got more prosperous, and they got a plank on each side of that, three plans running lengthways. And then they got still more settlers in, and they cut the planks all up into four foot lengths and made a four foot wide sidewalk. It only went down as far as Hazel Street for many years.

The ladies dresses came down so you could see just their toes sticking out. They were so long that they had to hold them up, get ahold of them and carry them, one hand for the dress, and the other hand would have to have an umbrella in it, if it was stormy weather. They were pretty well occupied getting along. And until they got the wider sidewalk, if a poor old man got in the road, he had to get off in the grass or the mud and let them get by. And they got so they used the sidewalk mostly in the afternoon. They would go up to town to do their purchasing. Their men went out in the evening, and no one could see what *they* were doing. They'd go out in the dark; there wasn't any ladies out then. They'd go up town to play cards and gamble. Trust them, they'd always find some back room they could get into.   [JK]

Improvements of all kinds

Soon after the turn of the century the appearance of this little wooden town started to change. Builders began using brick from the Clayburn mines on Sumas Mountain, or cement from the Elk Creek Cement Works. Now that the Fraser River dyking was completed, farmers and townsfolk alike could feel secure about their property. Nor was it long in being put to the test, as the highwater of the spring of 1902 was another of the big ones. On September 4th, 1907 the *Progress* was able to report, "The great prosperity and confidence which residents have in the future of the country are reflected by the progress of the town which is to-day growing faster than at any time since its foundation, and the many thousands of dollars being expended by citizens, new and old, in improvements of all kinds." That year the place acquired a new subdivision.

Then, in 1908, in response to a growing tension between the townspeople and the farming community, due to a conflict of interests, the town was split off from the municipality and became the city of Chilliwack. The next year they started building a city hall, a lovely little Palladian affair, for all the world like the summerhouse of some Italian nobleman—but cast in concrete. It was intended by its architect to be set in the midst of a city park, where it's peculiar charm could be displayed, and even today it's the city's most interesting building. That year they also built a large hotel and called it The Empress. Rollers were put under St. Thomas Anglican church, which had been occupying a valuable acre on one of the Five Corners, and a string of horses dragged it a few blocks to another site. In its place two buildings were erected, both made of concrete blocks.

1886   Typical of the development made in the Chilliwhack district during that period.   1903

The pioneer years were ending in a blaze of self-confidence. Already the modern era, as we like to think of it, was on its way. Chilliwack got its first waterworks in 1907, with water supplied from Elk Creek, and then, in 1908, its first telephone and electricity. Around that time the Yale Road was macadamized, and automobiles began to appear.

Clarke Brannick remembered "how the youngsters turned out from school to see the first automobile go by," driven by Captain Sam Gardner, a colourful Yukon riverboat navigator. Barely 30 years before, the children at the Indian school at Mission, hearing the toot of a whistle, had jumped out of their classroom window and run down through the orchard to see their first railway engine, and ride on it.

A carload of booze

One way of expressing the optimism of those days was to dream up a railway. But several schemes came and went before a serious beginning was made on a line to the Chilliwack Valley, one that would link the farming and logging communities with the coastal cities. It was actually a branch of the street railway system of Vancouver and New Westminster. The man in charge of construction was Fred Sinclair.

> It was standard equipment in those days. You couldn't use horse and scrapers because it was all timbered. The Scott Road to Cloverdale was heavily timbered. There was a strip of land at Surrey Centre, maybe a hundred acres, that was used for growing vegetables, and after we crossed the Serpentine [River] we would hit flats of cleared land. Then the lower part of Langley Prairie to Matsqui Prairie was all timbered, and all about the right size for railway ties. There was a contract let to a Chinaman in Victoria to furnish these ties, and he employed the cutters: they were Norwegians.
>
> You see, when we got to Huntingdon we were down on the flats and in the muskeg, and men were hard to get, good experienced construction men. They had had Norwegians. They're good workmen with scraper work, you know—shovel work. But my assistant engineer went over to the Canadian National in the canyon, and he employed these Norwegians and Swedes. A lot of them went over. So Bill Rennie asked me if he could put on Hindus. Well, they were sitting on the curb all over Vancouver, you know, starving to death—poor devils. They were up against it. And I said, "Now, as far as I'm concerned you can do it. If they're all right, all right. If they're not, we'll take them off. So we bought new wheelbarrows and took them out there. They come up from Huntingdon out to the Sumas River, and I went out to see how they started in.
>
> Well, they picked up the wheelbarrow, never put the wheel on it at all, carried it down into the barrow pit, loaded it up with a good big load of dirt, chunks of peat moss, then two of them boosted it up on to the Hindu's head. He walked up the plank and dumped it. But in a week they were good workmen—after they understood. They did use the wheel then.
>
> It wasn't a long job, you know. We laid track pretty fast. Along the Vedder Mountain was a little slow, but the last section was done in a year, so that when they started to operate the Electric hadn't been electrified. They were slow with that, and the first train was pulled with a locomotive.
>
> All the officials of the B.C. Electric were on the train, and all the reeves, the city officials from Westminster, and some from Vancouver, and Premier McBride and, I suppose, the cabinet, you know. And I was on it. And they had a carload of booze. [FS]

That was October 3rd, 1910, and it was a great civic occasion. The three coaches were festooned, and the town band was there to play 'Jolly Boys' and other lively airs.

> Premier McBride, he drove the last spike—gold spike. He couldn't hit it with a spike maul. The maul was too small and the spike was too small, and he struck at it two or three times. And then they got him a little bigger maul—carpenter's maul. The spike was plucked right away and presented to Dick McBride.   [FS]
>
> Dick McBride, I can remember him. We had turned out with the band. The train come in and they had a banquet over at St. Thomas' Hall, the English church hall, and the dignatories all went over there. We went over and played outside: we weren't invited inside, I remember that. We weren't altogether pleased about it, because some of the fellows, you know, had to quit their jobs to come in, and had to go back to work again.

With the coming of the valley's own railway, New Westminster could be reached in three hours, and people could go down and do their business and come back the same day. Doubtless there were some who still preferred a leisurely day's journey by riverboat to the rattle and rock of the trolleys, and their hard seats; so for them and their produce the steamboats maintained a regular service until 1913 when the new transcontinental railway started running along the south bank of the river. But in that age of buggies and democrats speed itself would have been an attraction, seeing the familiar farms go quickly by, and after them the shores of Sumas Lake, and the uncut timber that still covered so much of the country east of Matsqui.

> The B.C. Electric coming in really revolutionized the farming, because we used to have to ship our sour cream to the creamery, or make butter out of it. And when the B.C. Electric came in we all started shipping milk to Vancouver and Westminster. And instead of a few milk cows on some of the farms out here, there was quite large herds from then on.   [WF]

And they were in the fluid trade, in competition, of course, with the dairy farmers of the delta. Out of this eventually came the big milk cooperative, known as the Fraser Valley Milk Producers' Association.

But that's another story, because the pioneer days were over. In fact, even as far back as the 90s, the good valley land had all been preempted, and newcomers were having to buy or rent. Now, having reached the first decade of the twentieth century, the old originals could look back with a certain pride and satisfaction over the mere 40 years it had taken them to impress their life patterns on an "Eden" of hunters and gatherers. They had managed to transform it into, perhaps, the most fertile and productive corner of British Columbia, and the homeland of a reasonably harmonious community. In 1902 these old-timers got together at a dinner at the Harrison House and founded the Chilliwack Pioneer Society.

Someone who knew them has warned me not to put them on pedestals, implying that they were mere human beings with their normal quota of strengths and weaknesses, and that may well be so. But having made their acquaintance, so to speak, in other people's memories, I have come to see that they possessed precisely that strength of character and singleness of vision—even in their own day there were those who regarded them as narrow and overly religious—that was needed for what they had to do. Plainly, they were not your average gold miner. They brought with them, not only a pioneer inheritance, but a strong sense of values, they were looking for a place in which they could grow. They found it in this lovely valley, out on the prairies or in the clearings that they made. Here they discovered their own true West, where each was able to reach beyond the social and economic limitations of their upbringing.

What appears to be one of the valley's favourite stories concerns a certain Judge Bole of New Westminster and Mike Riley, Chilliwack's odd job man. The Judge had arrived from Ireland in 1877 and was the first lawyer to settle permanently on the mainland. Mike and his dog were equally well-known in their own circles. The dog, an old fox terrier, had gotten to be so fat that he waddled; and Mike, too, was getting on in years—a typical old Irishman, with a quick answer for everyone.

One day the judge was coming up the boardwalk from the Harrison House, when he caught up with Mike and his dog, and they walked along together. After a few minutes the judge ventured to remark, "I'll tell you, Mike, you'd be a long time in Ireland before you'd be seen walking up the street beside a judge."

"Begorry, yes!" says Mike. "And you, m'lud, would be a long time in Ireland before you became a judge."

Dock at Chilliwack Landing; cargo and livestock being loaded (PABC 73382).

Automobiles, Chilliwack Landing (PABC 88680).

John Ryder (PABC 43267).

Here comes Santa Claus

All this progress was not to everyone's taste. Every so often an old man would ride down out of the hills to appear in town, as if to remind everyone in the valley how far they had come. He'd been a Cariboo miner, and also one of the first freighters on the Cariboo Road. He was John Ryder, Cory and Jim Ryder's eldest brother. He had taken up a preemption on the Hope Slough and married, but when his sons were old enough to look after the place, he had moved up into the hills and was living by himself beside a little lake, which came to be known as Ryder Lake. Every now and then he'd come out for supplies, and to have a visit with his sister, Matilda Harrison. Although she did her best to persuade him to join the twentieth century, he professed to be supremely happy up there on his cloudy height, where he maintained he could grow the best apples and potatoes for miles around.

Whenever John Ryder came back into town he would ride his old white horse down this road, which was more of a trail than a road. And he was quite a picturesque figure. He had snow-white, curly hair, long curly whiskers, always beautifully clean. He wore a black overcoat, which I imagine at one time was a military coat. It came down as far as his knees. It didn't have any buttons, as far as I remember, but he kept it tied around his waist with a piece of rope. Quite often he didn't wear a hat. He had rosy cheeks, sat very straight in his saddle. And as he came down through the village the children would gather on the sidewalk and say, "Come on kids! Here comes Santa Claus!"   [NP]

Unidentified school children, South Sumas, 1889 (PABC 43220).

Sources

INTERVIEWS

The following interviews were used in the preparation of this issue of the SOUND HERITAGE SERIES:

CB   Clarke Brannick (1897–1967) youngest son of Joseph Brannick, who came from Owen Sound, Ontario in 1882. Interviewed in 1963 on the family farm, which he was still farming.

CEB   Charles E. Borden (1905–1978) late Professor Emeritus of Archaeology at the University of British Columbia. A leader in archaeological exploration and research in British Columbia for more than 30 years. Interviewed in the 1960s.

DM   Dan Milo (1864–1966) was a Chilliwack Indian and authority on native lore. Interviewed at Skowkale, near Sardis, in 1963.

FS   Fred Sinclair (1870–1964) surveyor and construction engineer for the Great Northern Railway and the B.C. Electric's line to Chilliwack. In charge of the draining of Sumas Lake after World War I. Interviewed in 1963.

FT   Fred Toop (1886–1976) youngest son of Sampson Toop, who came from Devonshire in 1872. As a teenager he took over his father's farm and ran it for 58 years. Interviewed in 1963.

FZ   Fred Zink (1896–1979) whose father, Jacob Zink, came from Germany and eventually bought a farm in the Lower Sumas area. Fred Zink's maternal grandfather was Henry Hall of the Royal Engineers. Interviewed in 1963.

HW   Horatio (Raish) Webb (1852–1936) was the son of John Webb, a prominent farmer of Marston Moretaine, Bedfordshire, England. Brother of Sarah Ashwell and Kate Mellard. Came out to New Westminster in the fall of 1869, and after a year helping his brother-in-law, G. R. Ashwell, he moved up to the Chilliwack Valley, and eventually bought land from A. C. Wells and settled at Sardis. He was the Chilliwack Valley's first historian with firsthand information on the early pioneer years. He died in 1936.

        HW-1 = *Chilliwack Progress,* 25 June, 1958.
        HW-2 = Letter from H. Webb to G. Brown, 31 July 1935; typed MS in PABC.

JF   John Fraser (b. 1892) whose father, Donald (Dan) Fraser took up a homestead near Abbotsford, and then became custom's officer at Huntingdon. Interviewed in 1963.

JH   Jack Henderson (1881–1974) son of John Calvin Henderson, storekeeper at Chilliwack Landing and later at Centreville. Played in the Chilliwack Brass Band for many years. Interviewed in 1963.

JK   James (Jim) Kipp (1886–1975) youngest son of Henry Kipp. Grew up on the family farm, now part of the city of Chilliwack. Interviewed in 1963.

JM   Jack McCutcheon (1880–1954) younger son of John McCutcheon, the Chilliwack Valley's pioneer telegraph agent. The family farm on the bank of the Chilliwack River has been absorbed by the city of Chilliwack. John McCutcheon's reminiscences were scribbled in three notebooks while he was in hospital for his last illness in 1954.

JS   Mrs. Joy Starr, born in the early 1890s. Daughter of William Fadden of Upper Sumas. Interviewed in 1963; at that time she had a diary of her mother's from which she read extracts pertinent to the 1894 flood.

KM   Mrs. Kate Mellard (1862–1965) widow of Sam Mellard, Chilliwack's second postmaster, sister of Horatio Webb and Sarah Ashwell. Arrived in Chilliwack in 1887 with her husband and daughters from Bedfordshire. Interviewed in 1963.

MS   Martin Starret (1888–1973) younger son of William Starret. Grew up on the family homestead at Silver Creek, just across from the island where Bill Bristol lived. Interviewed 1963–1969.

NM   Mrs. Norah Mercer (1881–1974) widow of Alec Mercer and youngest child of Jonathan Reece, who preempted land where the city of Chilliwack now stands in 1859. Interviewed in 1963.

NP   Mrs. Nellie Patriquin (1887–1976) daughter of Cory Ryder and niece of Mrs. Matilda Harrison. She took a great interest in local history, and was very helpful in various ways. Interviewed in 1963.

OW   Oliver Wells (1907–1970) son of Edwin Wells, the only son of A. C. Wells, who came into the valley in 1867. Oliver Wells was keenly interested in local history and Indian lore and language, and published pamphlets and articles in those fields. Interviewed in 1964.

RJ   Robert (Bob) Joe (1885–1970) was a Chilliwack Indian and historian of his people. Interviewed in 1963 at Tzeachton, south of Sardis.

RW   Ray Wells (b. 1894) son of Edwin Wells, and grandson of A. C. Wells. Interviewed in 1964.

WF   Win Fadden was born in the early 1890s. Son of William Fadden, who settled in Upper Sumas in 1885. Brother of Mrs. Joy Starr. Interviewed 1963.

WR   Mrs. Willena Reid, born about 1880. Daughter of Sam Nicholson of Mt. Lehman. Interviewed 1963.

Tapes of the interviews are held by the Sound and Moving Image Division, Provincial Archives of British Columbia.

BIBLIOGRAPHY

ARNETT, TERRANCE C. "The Chilliwack Valley Continuum: A Search for a Canadian Land Ethic," [M. Arch.] thesis, UBC, 1976.

COOK, DONNA H. "Early Settlement in the Chilliwack Valley," [thesis] Department of Geography, UBC, 1979.

CROSBY, THOMAS *Among the An-ko-me-nums,* Toronto, William Biggs, 1907.

EVANS, C. H. *Chilliwack Pioneer Ladies,* Chilliwack, *Chilliwack Progress,* 1915.

FRASER, SIMON *The Letters and Journals of Simon Fraser 1806–1808,* W. Kaye Lamb, Ed., Toronto, the Macmillan Co. of Canada Ltd., 1966.

HUDSON BAY COMPANY "Journal of the Voyage from Fort Vancouver to Fraser's River and of the Establishment of Fort Langley . . . 1827–1830," typewritten MS, PABC, Victoria.

HUTCHINGS & ROSENFIELD Hutching's Illustrated Magazine, San Francisco, 1859.

LORD, JOHN KEAST *The Naturalist in Vancouver Island and British Columbia,* two vols., London, Richard Bentley, 1866.

WEBB, HORATIO "Chilliwhack Valley and its Pioneers," typewritten MS, PABC.

WELLS, OLIVER, N. *A. C. Wells,* A Biography, Np., Np., January 20, 1963.

WELLS, OLIVER, N. *A Vocabulary of Native Words in the Halkomelem Language,* Sardis, Np., 1965. *Myths and Legends of the Staw-loh Indians of South Western British Columbia,* Np., Np., 1970.

WILSON, CHARLES "Journal of Service of Lieutenant Charles William Wilson, R. E. with Boundary Commission, April 20, 1858–June 11, 1860", Vol. 1. Typewritten MSS, PABC, Victoria.

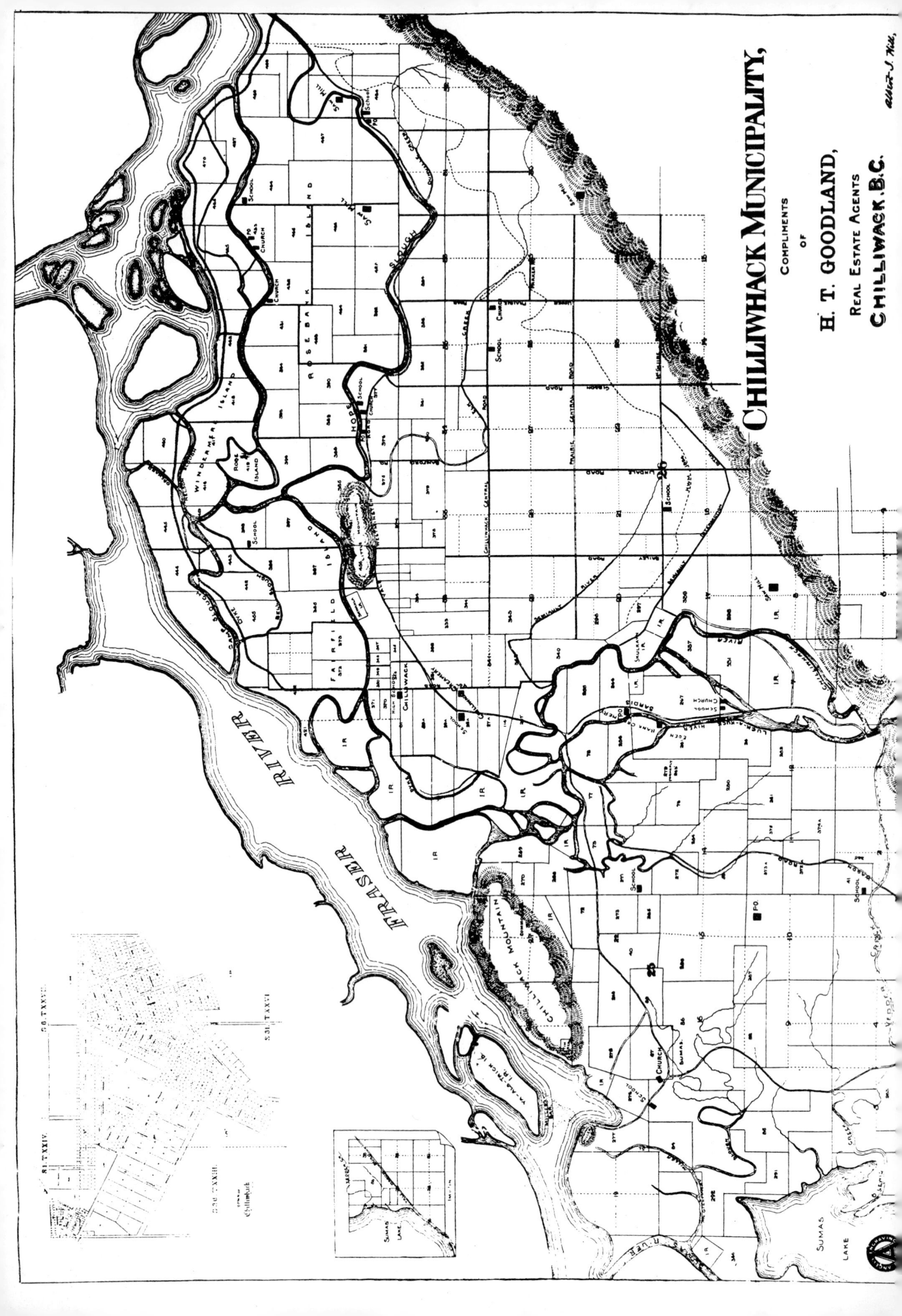

PHOTO CREDITS

The McCutcheon Family: pp. 69 and 76.

All other photographs from the Visual Records Division of the Provincial Archives of British Columbia.

MAP CREDITS

Library and Maps Section, Provincial Archives of British Columbia.

DESIGN

Charles Lillard and David Mattison

SOUND HERITAGE SERIES

Provincial Archives of British Columbia
Victoria, B.C., Canada V8V 1X4

SOUND HERITAGE SERIES, upcoming issues .... $14 for four numbers
(by prepaid subscription)

No. 38   IMAGINE PLEASE: Early Radio Broadcasting in British Columbia
by Dennis J. Duffy.
Cassette Sound Program, $2.50.

No. 39   TALL TALES OF BRITISH COLUMBIA
by Michael Taft.
Cassette Sound Program, $2.50.

No. 40   GROWING UP IN THE VALLEY (working title).
Children growing up in the Fraser Valley before WW I
by Imbert Orchard.
Cassette Sound Program, $2.50.

SOUND HERITAGE SERIES BACKLIST

No. 37   FLOODLAND AND FOREST $4.50
Memories of the Chilliwack Valley by Imbert Orchard, 88 pp.

No. 36   DREAMS OF FREEDOM: BELLA COOLA, CAPE SCOTT, SOINTULA,
88 pp. $4.50
Cassette Sound Program, $2.50.

No. 35   EXTRA! WHEN THE PAPERS HAD THE ONLY NEWS $4.50
Stories of British Columbia's Daily Papers
Cassette Sound Program, *Such Interesting People*, $2.50.

No. 34   NOW YOU ARE MY BROTHER: MISSIONARIES IN BRITISH
COLUMBIA $4.50
by Margaret Whitehead, 92 pp.

No. 33   SETTLING CLAYOQUOT $4.50
Vancouver Island's West Coast, 76 pp.
Cassette Sound Program, *Castle Island and Other Stories of Clayoquot
Sound*, $2.50.

No. 32   WHERE THE LARDEAU RIVER FLOWS $4.50
Recollections of the Kootenay Region, 84 pp.
Cassette Sound Program, *Legends of the Lardeau: The Stories of Red
McLeod and Andy Daney*, $2.50.

No. 31   RAILROADERS $4.50
Recollections of the Steam Era on British Columbia's Railroads.
Cassette Sound Program, *Avalanche Mountain*, $2.50.

No. 30   MARTIN — THE STORY OF A YOUNG FUR TRADER $4.50
The northern reminiscences of Martin Starret, 76 pp.
Cassette Sound Programs, *Travellers of the North* and *The Childhood of
Martin Starret*, $2.50 each.

No. 29   SEASON'S GREETINGS FROM BRITISH COLUMBIA'S PAST $4.50
Christmas as celebrated by British Columbia residents, 1880–1930, 74 pp.
Cassette Sound Program, *Sounds of Christmas Past*, $2.50.

No. 28   THE MAGNIFICENT DISTANCES $4.50
Early Aviation in British Columbia, 1910–1940, 78 pp.
Cassette Sound Program, *From Jericho Beach to Swanson Bay*, $2.50.

No. 27   IN THE WESTERN MOUNTAINS $4.50
    Early Mountaineering in British Columbia, 76 pp.
    Cassette Sound Program, *Mountaineering at the Coast,* $2.50.
No. 26   BRIGHT SUNSHINE AND A BRAND NEW COUNTRY $4.50
    Recollections of Life in the Okanagan Valley, 1890–1914, 80 pp.
    Cassette Sound Program, *Paddy Acland's Progress,* $2.50.
Nos. 24 and 25   OPENING DOORS $9.00
    Stories of the ethnic immigrants to Vancouver's East End, 186 pp.
No. 23   FIGHTING FOR LABOUR $4.50
    Four decades of work in British Columbia, 78 pp.
    Cassette Sound Program, *Four Decades, Four Strikes,* $2.50.
No. 22   A VICTORIAN TAPESTRY $4.50
    Recollections and stories about the City of Victoria, 1890–1914, 76 pp.
    Cassette Sound Program, *In the House of the Old Doctor,* $2.50.
No. 21   NU•TKA• The History and Survival of Nootkan Culture $4.50
    A 4,000-year history of the Nootkans at Yuquot and a description of the survival of
    Nootkan culture, 65 pp.
    Cassette Sound Program, *Salmon People from Under the Sea,* $2.50.
No. 20   NU•TKA• Captain Cook and The Spanish Explorers on the Coast $4.50
    The early contact between Europeans and the Nootka Indians including
    traditional stories of the Nootka Indians, 101 pp.
    Cassette Sound Program, *Landfall on Unknown Seas,* $2.50.
No. 19   TOIL AND PEACEFUL LIFE $4.50
    Doukhobors of the West Kootenays recall their struggles in Russia and their life in
    Canada, 78 pp.
No. 18   MEN OF THE FOREST $4.50
    Writings about life and work in the forests of British Columbia, 78 pp.
No. 16   LILLOOET STORIES $4.50
    Traditional myths, stories and legends of the Lillooet Indians, 78 pp.
    Cassette Sound Program, *Lillooet Stories,* $2.50.
No. 14   MYTH AND THE MOUNTAINS $4.50
    Creative writing based on British Columbia's spoken traditions, 45 pp.

Robert Imbert Orchard was born in Canada in 1909 and educated in England. He has been, at various times, actively engaged in theatre, teaching, broadcasting and regional history. Orchard first came to British Columbia in 1942 and with the exception of nine years spent at the University of Alberta establishing a theatre studies program, he has been here ever since. He worked for the CBC in Vancouver, first as a script editor and later as a radio producer specializing in programs about the early days in the province. These were based on numerous interviews with its old-timers, and involving travelling with a tape recorder, not only by car, but by small plane, pack horse, barge, riverboat and freight boat. Imbert Orchard retired from the CBC in 1974.

Imbert Orchard is the author of one previous issue in the Sound Heritage Series, *Martin: The Story of a Young Fur Trader* (*SHS* No. 30).

Queen's Printer for British Columbia ©
Victoria, 1983